HOMETOWN ASYLUM

A HISTORY AND MEMOIR OF INSTITUTIONAL CARE

JACK MARTIN

Suite 300 - 990 Fort St
Victoria, BC, V8V 3K2
Canada

www.friesenpress.com

ISBN
978-1-5255-8974-4 (Hardcover)
978-1-5255-8973-7 (Paperback)
978-1-5255-8975-1 (eBook)

1. PSYCHOLOGY, HISTORY

Distributed to the trade by The Ingram Book Company

CONTENTS

To all who truly care for those experiencing mental disorders.
Yours is a difficult and noble calling.

ACKNOWLEDGEMENTS

I thank those who provided information and were willing to take the time to talk to me while I researched and wrote this book. In particular, the kind and generous assistance provided by Sandy Allsopp (Museum Curator, Fort Ostell Museum in Ponoka, Alberta) was invaluable. Without her help and guidance, this book never would have been written. The archivists and staff at the Provincial Archives of Alberta in Edmonton were also most helpful, as were those who guided me in accessing and viewing reports and editorials in several Alberta newspaper archives and micro-fiche repositories. The same can be said about others who assisted me in accessing Hansard transcriptions and other relevant materials in the Library of the Legislative Assembly of Alberta in Edmonton. Finally, I thank my wife Wyn, daughter Kara, and friends Jeff Sugarman and Jim Sanders for reading and commenting on drafts of the manuscript. Another good friend, Mel Auten, assisted me in combing through and making notes about materials located in the Provincial Archives of Alberta. Others to whom I am very grateful are mentioned in various footnotes included throughout what follows.

Asylum is a Latin word meaning "sanctuary." Its literal meaning is "an inviolable place." The contemporary meaning of the word dates from 1773 and refers to "a benevolent institution to shelter some class of persons suffering social, mental or bodily disorders."

CHAPTER ONE:
BEGINNINGS

Have you ever imagined having a mental illness? Probably not, at least in any detail, unless you or someone close to you has been affected directly. It is not easy to envision what suffering a mental illness might entail, unless you are somehow immersed in the lives of those afflicted. There is no substitute for close and direct experience. Such experience was easily obtained during my childhood, so much so that when I once wondered aloud why I had become a psychologist, my daughter laughingly remarked, "What else could you possibly have become"? I assume and hope she was not referencing what she perceives as gaps in my character that would have prevented other possibilities, but referring instead to the large psychiatric institution and its residents that populated so many of my childhood, adolescent and early adult experiences. If she also had in mind my life with my parents, she probably makes a pretty strong case.

This is a book that is both a history and a memoir. In it, I tell the story of the Alberta Hospital Ponoka, or AHP. For many years during the first and middle parts of the twentieth century, the AHP was the largest and most populated psychiatric institution in the Western Canadian Province of Alberta. That it also was located on the outskirts of my hometown, and my father was employed there, meant that its historical story interacted with my own life experience. Herein, I explore and tell some of the Hospital's history and some of my own, growing up in Ponoka in my youth, and in my later career as a professional and academic psychologist. By linking the history of the Hospital to parts of my history, I hope to inject personal experiences and perspectives into my narrative that might resonate with readers' own life experiences and help give the stories I tell greater interest. Although both stories, that of the Hospital and my own, are local and particular, I hope their interaction provides a metaphorical site or vantage point from which the reader might perceive and be inclined to think more about mental illness and the treatment of those suffering it. In other words, I wish the local and particular to open to a much broader consideration of past and contemporary issues in mental health service and treatment from the perspectives of those receiving them, those attempting to provide them, and members of the general public whose tax dollars and attitudes inevitably contribute to the treatment and care of those with mental disorders. To locate and enhance my narrative, I provide some local and wider social, cultural, political and economic context to assist readers to imagine and position themselves within the times and places I describe, and within the history of psychiatry, psychology, and institutional care more generally. Embedded within the overall narrative are histories and analyses of a wide array of different and ever-changing treatments for mental disorders that include, not only particular approaches such as shock treatments, psychopharmaceuticals and psychotherapies, but also wider debates concerning psychiatry, deinstitutionalization, and the personal and societal costs and challenges of mental illness.

• • •

My extended family often met at Gull Lake at least once during the hot days of the Central Alberta summers of my youth. As an only child, my cousins were as close to siblings as I had, except for a few good friends in the neighbourhood and at school. During those summer days at the lake, I solidified my sense of family by running wild with my cousins in the water, along the sandy beaches, and among the dunes. We played childhood games and invented routines and stories of our own—reveling in our freedom and each others' company. My uncles and aunts, like my parents, had the good sense to let us roam as long as we checked in at mealtimes and were back at the campsite by dusk. (These were different times from those many face now.)

I was of interest to my cousins as one of the oldest of us, and for the reputation of my hometown, a place different from theirs because of the large mental hospital that sprawled to the south of the rural town of Ponoka, near the Ponoka Golf Club—a place where you could locate patients of the hospital on eternal searches for lost golf balls they might find in the woods and sell for pennies to the golfers, one of the few means of making money available to those fortunate enough to be granted day paroles. There was a rumour when I was young that a patient from the hospital had built a shack somewhere in the woods of the course, and my pals and I often looked for it when also searching for wayward balls, but to no avail. Yet apparently the story was true, for I discovered when researching this book that a patient had burned to death in just such a shack, an event that set off one of the many investigations of patient monitoring and treatment at the Hospital over the course of its history.

As if to solidify my status as unique and interesting, my father, who worked at the Hospital as a baker, sometimes brought along a patient or two to our lake gatherings. Hospital staff were encouraged to take patients to their homes and family outings as a way of counteracting the communal strangeness of patients' daily lives with others like themselves, something hospital psychologists later referred to as "normalization." As kids, we took careful note of these strangers, trying to figure out exactly how they were crazy, and how they hopefully differed greatly from ourselves. We regaled each other with the story of the time when a tall man, who shuffled his feet and leaned forward as if he might fall at any time face-first into the beach, sat down by the water's edge and undressed entirely, revealing an enormous penis that swung liberally as he got up and continued his walk. Another time, while one of my younger cousins and I watched, a patient working in our home garden suddenly began to speak loudly and gesture adamantly to the raspberry bushes. Such events, when codified into brief rubrics we invented for them, could send us into gales of giggles for days, and even now sometimes warrant reminiscence.

However, what was fun and funny with family was anything but when meeting people whose only knowledge of Ponoka was its famous Hospital. For years, when asked where I was from, I would say I grew up just north of Red Deer, having tired of the line of banter that inevitably followed full admission of place and origin. I now sometimes try to imagine what it might have been like if I had been, or said I'd been, a patient myself. To this day, one of the great things about meeting others from Ponoka is the comforting sense that we are in this thing together. Even now, some fifty years since I worked at the Hospital as a temporary orderly during a couple of summers while attending the University of Alberta, stories about the Hospital can make up a good portion of reminiscences with high school classmates at occasional reunions and other get-togethers.

In my youth, actual distance from the hospital was something that spoke directly to one's status in the town of Ponoka. Unfortunately for those of us whose parents lived and worked at the Hospital, this way of seeing things did not work to our benefit. The only exceptions were the psychiatrists or hospital administrators, whose titles and degrees excused them and their families from being situated in this way. As a child, I met several of the psychiatrists through their children, my parents and neighbours. However, I had little sense of how nationally and internationally distinguished several of them were. It still strikes me as odd that some of the most renowned psychiatrists in the country lived on the other side of the golf course that separated our street from the Hospital.

• • •

The Insane Asylum at Ponoka or the Ponoka Hospital for the Insane, later renamed as the Provincial Mental Hospital (in 1923) and later still as the Alberta Hospital Ponoka (in 1964),[1] was opened in 1911, four years after a decree passed by the recently formed Alberta Government entitled the "Insanity Act" enabled the Lieutenant-Governor in Council to make arrangements to build it.[2] Two years earlier, in 1905, Alberta was organized as a Province, distinguishing itself from its previous identity as part of the vast Canadian Northwest Territory. During that time, any cases of insanity within what would become the new Province's boundaries had been shipped off to take up residence in the asylums of Manitoba, especially those in the communities of Selkirk and Brandon, the latter institution commonly known as "The Mental." As originally envisioned, the Asylum at Ponoka was to be the first of several small, advanced care facilities where patients would receive personalized attention in a peaceful and arresting rural environment. However, things did not work out this way, and it became the largest mental health facility in the province of Alberta for most of the twentieth century. It was restructured into the Centennial Centre for Mental Health and Brain Injury shortly into the twenty-first century.

---

1   Herein, I mostly use the terms "Alberta Hospital Ponoka (AHP)," "Ponoka Hospital," "Provincial Mental Hospital (PMH)" or simply "the Hospital" interchangeably, for ease and convenience, although when referring to particular documents and relevant legislation, I will use the formal name of the Hospital as contained in those documents.

2   Secondary source materials about the early days of the Asylum at Ponoka in this chapter include: Julius Johnson et al. (1986). *A history of dedication and caring: 75 years serving Alberta 1911-1986*. Ponoka: Alberta Hospital Ponoka; Ronald, A. LaJeunesse (2002). *Political Asylums*. Edmonton, AB: Muttart Foundation; Earl E. Roberts (1973). *Ponoka Panorama* (pp. 191-240). Ponoka, AB: Ponoka and District Historical Society; Alexandra Whittick (2015). "An overview of policy and practice in Alberta's first mental hospital." In A. Loewenau, K. Lucyk, and F. W. Stahnisch (Eds.), *The Proceedings of the 20th Anniversary History of Medicine Days Conference 2011*. Lady Stephenson Library, Newcastle Upon Tyne, UK: Cambridge Scholars Publishing.

I am interested in and know some of these things because in the latter part of my professional and academic life, I gave up applied psychology (mostly educational and counselling psychology and psychotherapy), and took up the history and theory of psychology. During the fifteen years prior to my retirement from the Department of Psychology at Simon Fraser University, I taught a mandatory class in the history of psychology to large cohorts of mostly, but not exclusively, young people who typically were not enamoured of history. To spice things up and hold their attention, I made it a practice also to include bits and pieces drawn from the history of psychiatry into my lectures, a strategy that now pays dividends when writing this book.

• • •

The first asylum in North America was opened in the basement of the Philadelphia Hospital in 1751, followed a few years later by the first stand-alone asylum, which was constructed in Virginia. It wasn't until some sixty years later that the first asylum in Canada opened in 1835 in St. John, New Brunswick. Prior to the "asylum age," those with mental health difficulties were cared for in their homes or subjected to the hardships of poorhouses, workhouses or jails. The word "asylum" was used by British mental health reformers like Robert Gardner Hill and John Conolly as a replacement for the word "madhouse." Conolly's use of "asylum" was intended to signify the kind of attentive and respectful care he advocated. Appointed as superintendent of London's famous Bedlam Madhouse in 1839, Conolly abhorred the methods of physical restraint, punishment and bloodletting, the stale and foul air, and the overcrowding and unsanitary conditions of the madhouse. Within five years, he succeeded in greatly reducing the use of restraining devices like straightjackets and strapped armchairs, and provided inmates with water to wash with, decent clothes and rooms with ventilation and heat. Conolly was among the first practitioners of what came to be called "moral treatment," in which patients were to be cared for with as much kindness as their conditions allowed.[3]

For many years thereafter, aspects of the traditional Bedlam approach coupled with aspects of moral treatment would be the standard in most Canadian asylums. For example, at "The Mental," during the time it housed the Alberta area's sick, there was considerable kindness, solicitude, food and warmth but there were also patients who were restrained in straitjackets, locked in cupboards, strapped and caged on beds, and shackled with chains. Even in my own experience as a temporary institutional attendant at Ponoka during the summers of 1968 and 1969, I was shocked by how quickly cruelties could be administered in an otherwise caring context when patients acted in ways that were viewed as aggressive or disgusting. In such circumstances, a towel being used to dry a patient fresh from a bath might suddenly be snapped at the patient when he began to fondle himself or a helping hand might tighten and strike if its owner reacted to being unexpectedly pushed. The tipping point depended greatly on the character and mood of the caregivers, and more generally on institutional factors such as levels of funding, crowding and the inclinations and inducements of political and medical officials.

• • •

Ponoka (an English version of the Blackfoot Nation's word "ponokaii" for "Elk," an animal depicted on the town's flag) was incorporated in 1904. During the Spring of 1800, if early April can be called Spring in Alberta, the explorer David Thompson was the first non-aboriginal visitor to the area that the town of Ponoka later would occupy. Thompson and his party, guided by a member of the Blackfoot Nation,

---

3   Historical information such as in the first part of this paragraph is taken from lecture notes and background material I collected over many years of teaching courses on counselling, psychotherapy, and the history of psychology at Simon Fraser University and what was then called The University of Western Ontario (now Western University).

followed the Battle River that now runs through the town of Ponoka from south to north, and flows just to the west of the land on which the Alberta Hospital was constructed. The river's name derives from the 18th century rivalry between the Blackfoot and Cree peoples. Many years later, during the 1940s, a patient of the hospital on a day pass rescued a local youth who almost drowned in the River near the spot where Thompson crossed it. When the Canadian Pacific Railroad arrived in 1895, the town site was known simply as "Siding 14," now a popular moniker for several businesses near the north walking bridge and a recently installed brew pub in the burgeoning industrial park area of the town. By the 1960s, Ponoka had grown to a community of approximately 4,000 people, serving the needs of both residents and a surrounding area populated by farmers and ranchers, a heritage celebrated by the annual Ponoka Stampede in early July, currently described by town officials on the municipality's website as "seven full days of rodeo action attracting the best two and four-legged rodeo athletes in the world." However, despite its rural, agrarian reputation, for most of the town's history, the primary employer for those who earned a living in Ponoka was the Alberta Hospital. The much-heralded local Stampede was one of many occasions during which patients from the Hospital who enjoyed "day privileges" could be found sitting, together with a few nurses and orderlies, amongst town folk and visitors. During the time I worked briefly at the Hospital in the summers of 1968 and 1969, I was frequently impressed by the general absence of emotional outbursts or unusual behaviour from patients on such occasions. When such acts did occasionally occur, they tended mostly to be taken in stride, at least by the local Ponokans in attendance.

· · ·

Work on the construction of the Hospital began on August 1, 1908. The design was essentially that of the psychiatric hospital in Utica, New York. Built entirely of fireproof materials (mostly Calgary sandstone and red brick) when it opened in 1911, the Hospital consisted of a central administration building flanked by "wings" (one for men, the other for women) and intended to house a total of 150 patients. Three stories and a basement extended across the entire structure. The central building was connected to a separate powerhouse by a tunnel and also included a full laundry. A water tower with a tank capacity of 80,000 gallons was supplied with water from a well 200 feet deep. A series of concrete, live-earth beds, all covered (and hidden) by a frame and plantings, treated sewage before it was discharged into the surrounding countryside and eventually drained into the Battle River.

Viewed from the front, a rock-faced, coarse sandstone basement extended around and provided the foundation for the three-story brick structure, interrupted by a main entrance porch and smaller porches leading into each of the wings. The entire structure was topped with a high cement-plastered, buff-coloured frieze with a large overhanging cornice, just below a low-pitched roof. Central steam heating and electrical lighting were available throughout the building, which was located on the rolling hills of the Alberta parkland, atop fertile agricultural land and nicely situated to command a magnificent view of the surrounding countryside. The property included 2,391 acres, much of which became cultivated farmland, grounds and gardens devoted to Hospital use. Situated between the higher-cost population centres of Calgary and Edmonton on the Canadian Pacific Railway line, the cost of care was estimated at fifty cents per day per patient, exactly half the cost of care at the Brandon Asylum. This first building and its powerhouse, now designated as a "heritage building," are the only structures that remain of what, by the 1970s, included a sprawling warren of additional buildings to house patients and supply the Hospital with the services and supplies it required.

The establishment of the Insane Asylum at Ponoka was a coup for Provincial Agriculture Minister Duncan McLean Marshall, whose portfolio included mental health. Marshall, who had been lobbied by a group of Ponokans led by Dr. W. A. Campbell to locate the facility near Ponoka, assured Alberta Premier A. C. Rutherford and his government colleagues that this would be a model institution, employing progressive moral treatments as practiced in the best asylums anywhere in the world. Marshall foresaw a place of solitude, escape and comfort in a stress-free, healthy and pastoral environment in which patients might relax, learn to manage their difficulties and come to live "normally" within a family-like, loving and tolerant society. Provincial Secretary A. J. McLean was tasked with visiting and interviewing applicants for the position of Medical Superintendent at Ponoka. Sharing Marshall's belief that patients would benefit greatly from positive exposure to peaceful and caring social situations, he determined that Dr. Thomas Dawson, originally from Edinburgh, Scotland, was exactly the right man for the job. Clearly impressed with the new Hospital's sophisticated technology, Dawson enthused, "Ornamental electric lamps exist everywhere, indeed there is an air of luxuriance and comfort when all the lights are aglow, which should aid in dispelling doubt and gloom; nor are we hiding our light under a bushel but delivering it to Ponoka, which lies in semi-darkness about one and a half miles distant to the northwest...There is a complete system of telephonic communication throughout the building."[4] All in all, the original atmosphere of the Hospital was such that visitors could see many of the comforts of home in the rooms occupied by patients. No isolated enclosures were constructed in the Hospital's interior and none were used in the earliest days of the Hospital's history.

Unfortunately, Marshall and McLean's idyllic vision was derailed almost immediately after the Hospital opened. Newly elected premier Arthur Lewis Sifton was of the opinion that the Province's finances could not support Marshall's vision of a network of small, familial facilities at Ponoka and similar operations proposed for several other Provincial sites. Expanding and centralizing the Ponoka Asylum made much more financial and administrative sense to Sifton and his cabinet.

---

4   As quoted in Julius Johnson et al. (1986). *A history of dedication and caring: 75 years serving Alberta 1911-1986*. Ponoka: Alberta Hospital Ponoka, p. 2.

Consequently, plans were already being made by the new Provincial Government to expand and build additional structures at Ponoka at roughly the same time that the Hospital first opened its doors.

• • •

The first annual report filed by Dr. Dawson, the well-liked and highly respected former Medical Health officer of the City of Calgary who had been selected to head the new Hospital as its Medical Superintendent, was submitted to the Government of Alberta through its Deputy Provincial Secretary, on January 12, 1912.[5] The report stated "the Provincial Hospital for the Insane at Ponoka was opened for patients on July 4th, 1911." The patient population for the first year of operation already exceeded the intended 150 patient limit, totaling 192 (134 men and 58 women), 164 of whom were transferred from the mental hospital at Brandon, Manitoba. Ten of the transferred patients, all deemed chronic and incurable, were very debilitated, bed-ridden and never recovered from their transfer, dying shortly following their arrival at Ponoka. After reporting this information, Dawson goes on to laud "the fine situation and pure air [of the new Hospital and its environs] combined with the structural arrangements for comfort and modern appliances for treatment [mostly facilities for hydrotherapy]." He also noted the urgent need for a mortuary and a post mortem facility with a pathology room so that each body can be examined thoroughly to determine cause of death and "where in time pathological research work could be done."

---

5   Annual reports prepared for the Alberta Provincial Government by the Medical Superintendents of the Ponoka Hospital from 1911 to 1929 constitute the major primary sources for the material in this chapter. These reports may be found in the Provincial Archives of Alberta, Edmonton AB and the Fort Ostell Museum and Archives, Ponoka, AB. Unless otherwise indicated, all material enclosed in quotation marks in this chapter is from one or other of these reports.

However, the need for a mortuary was not only legal, ethical and medical, it also signified the fact that the Hospital itself was a community in which all the usual community functions needed to be available. As in other communities, residents lived and died, and the physical spaces and tools to support living and dying, and the customs surrounding both, were essential.

• • •

Many years later when I was employed as a temporary attendant at the Hospital, I was working night shifts so that I also could take a course in abnormal psychology at the University of Alberta offered early on Tuesday and Thursday mornings. One night a patient passed away in his sleep, and I was given the responsibility of moving his body to a trolley and rolling him down to the Hospital morgue. As I made the final, long sloping descent to the basement facility, I still can recall being overcome by a strongly felt but puzzling sense of affinity with the deceased patient, a man with whom I had spoken and interacted on only a few brief occasions. While walking him down that ramp, I felt linked to him as another person who had shared the particularly human condition of living in the face of death, one that I and every other person faces and experiences until we, too, are gone. I recall taking particular care to place him carefully and respectfully where he needed to be located and hovering over him for several minutes after I had done so. Perhaps Kierkegaard was on to something when he wrote about a sense of transcendent belonging that arises in the midst of all our fear, trembling and suffering.

• • •

Elsewhere in his first annual report, Dawson described the successful operation of the Hospital Farm, reporting good crops of oats, potatoes and carrots, as well as an ample supply of milk from twenty-one milch cows. Throughout the first fifty years of its history, the Hospital existed as a mostly self-sufficient operation, providing food, electricity, water and other necessities of life to its patients and staff. In its first year of operation, patient labour was supplied by twenty male patients who worked on the farm, eight who worked in the kitchen, four in the laundry, three in the boiler house and forty who assisted with work on the wards. In addition, several women patients were engaged in sewing and mending, three more worked in the laundry, two in the kitchen and twelve assisted in ward work. The extent to which patient labour was therapeutic, and the extent to which it was exploitive was to become a continuing debate amongst Hospital staff, administrators, external assessors and commentators and patients themselves.

• • •

The years from 1912 to 1919 are sometimes referred to in Hospital lore as "the pioneering years," and coincided with the earliest years of my father and mother, who were born in 1913 and 1917 respectively. By the 1940s, my father's life and the history of the Alberta Hospital Ponoka had begun to intersect in ways that were later to furnish many of my earliest memories and experiences during the 1950s and 1960s. Born into an extended family that included many siblings, to parents whose families had immigrated to southern Alberta by way of Germany with a detour through Russia, my father left school at an early age to work on the family farm. The premature death of his father, my paternal grandfather, was attributed to the post World War I Spanish influenza, a disease that also infected 266 patients at the Alberta Hospital Ponoka and killed twenty-nine of them, along with two staff members. After years of struggling to keep the farm afloat, and to get along with his uncle, who had taken control of all family holdings when my grandfather died, my father began to look for other options. His search eventually led him, together with his new wife, to Ponoka as one of the non-patient farmers at the Alberta Hospital in the late 1930s.

My mother had met my father while working as a single-classroom, multi-grade schoolteacher in the small hamlet of Enchant, Alberta, where she had taken her first teaching job after graduating at a surprisingly young age from the Normal School in Camrose, Alberta. A gifted mathematician, my mother was not allowed by her father to study mathematics at the University of Alberta, because he viewed such a venture and venue as inappropriate for a young woman. When my parents moved to Ponoka, she worked as a teacher while he farmed as an employee of the Hospital. My mother's parents also were farmers, although their main income came from my grandfather's job as a schoolteacher in Hughenden, Alberta. My maternal grandmother was active in a variety of community groups, especially the Women's Institute of Alberta, which was heavily involved in advancing health care, including mental health, in the Province.

• • •

By the time my parents arrived in Ponoka, the Hospital had changed a great deal from its debut in 1911. During the "pioneer days" of the decade following its establishment, it grew rapidly in patient population, buildings and facilities that ensured its self-sufficiency. Given a continuing influx of admissions, a new four-story building (Parkside) for male patients was completed in 1912. The same year also saw the construction of two six-room brick cottage residences for the medical superintendent and the bursar, as well as a house for the farm manager, and three duplex cottages to accommodate staff who had been living in tents since the institution first opened its doors. By 1914, Superintendent Dawson had acquired his mortuary and post-mortem facilities and in 1915, a new three-story edifice for females was constructed; it was named Lawncrest. By 1919, further expansion of facilities included a new admissions building for male patients, two new male wards and two new female wards, as well as a new kitchen, bakeshop and root house. Other extensions to the Hospital's physical plant were a somewhat successful gas well, following a dry one, the breaking and cultivation of additional farmland, and the construction of pigsties, a cow barn and a grain silo. Because gas pressure from the new well was prone to fluctuation, the Hospital returned to the use of coal until 1948, when gas was piped directly to the facility by Northwestern Utilities.

Dr. Dawson adopted a humanistic perspective that viewed his patients as social beings who could benefit from interpersonal interaction and exposure to pleasant surroundings. In his annual reports from 1912 to 1916, he describes efforts to provide music to accompany patient meals, sometimes supplied by a small staff orchestra during dinner, dayrooms in the new buildings that were "large and cheerful, and, on account of the southern aspect, bright and sunny" and activities like billiards, football (soccer), and outside work for the "better patients." In 1914, patients watched their first film—a 35 mm production in which a Red Cross nurse promoted the sale of World War I savings bonds. In his 1913 and 1915 reports, Dawson describes structural changes to existing wards and new floor plans that "made a great difference to both patients and nurses" in that "patients look much better and are less noisy and disturbed and are happier and more easily managed." These included "bath-rooms...fit for any first-class hotel" and recreation areas that "look very pretty when lit up." "It adds greatly to the contentment of patients to live in clean and bright wards."

Overall, Dawson's approach to patient care was progressive and aligned with the ideal of moral treatment to combine healthy patient activity and social interactivity within a tranquil environment. His strong belief in the healing powers of pleasant surroundings, physical activity, cultural exposure and social interactivity was also combined with considerable administrative capability—evident in the introduction of more efficient procedures designed to reduce patient mortality and recovery rates by ensuring minimal delay between the onset of their illnesses and their admission to the hospital and in his skillful deployment and scheduling of Hospital staff to ensure smooth and effective institutional functioning. However, even with all his considerable good will and skill, Dr. Dawson experienced considerable frustration with an ever-increasing influx of new patients and a Provincial approach to mental health that was inconsistent, and at times contradictory.

• • •

The Provincial Government continued to oscillate on its long-term mental health strategy. Many in the Provincial Legislature favoured a traditionally large, all-purpose facility. However, influential members of the Government like Duncan Marshall, Minister of Agriculture, and high powered consultants like Dr. Clarence Hincks, who had founded the Canadian National Committee for Mental Hygiene after struggling with depression himself, continued to argue for the more progressive alternative of several smaller hospitals scattered throughout the Province to enhance accessibility and limit what they regarded as undesirable effects induced by large-scale institutional care. Both argued that a patient-oriented approach to care within supportive, locally accessible treatment centres would enhance the possibility of patient rehabilitation and re-entry into productive everyday life in surrounding communities. However, for financial reasons, concerns about efficiency, and perhaps because a main worry of most legislators was the incarceration and removal of "psychologically dangerous" individuals from normal society, the decision eventually was to opt for the large institutional model, supported by a smaller number of more specialized facilities, most of which were planned but not built. A few such facilities were eventually constructed, but at a much more leisurely pace than was required by the large and steadily increasing numbers of people being committed for treatment or voluntarily requesting it. The result was a rather slap-dash approach to expanding mental health facilities only when absolutely necessary, and without a coherent, overall plan for the delivery of services to those suffering from mental disorders. The recommendations of Marshall and Hincks for a sufficient number of small psychopathic hospitals throughout the Province were lost in the cost controlling efficiency of the bureaucracy.

Hincks, in his capacity as Head of the Canadian National Committee for Mental Hygiene, was greatly disappointed by the direction taken by the Alberta Government. He was to be even more disturbed when, after serving for five years, Superintendent Dawson was replaced by Dr. Edelston Harvey Cooke in 1916 as Medical Superintendent of the Ponoka Hospital. Hincks and Cooke represented dramatically different sides of the "traditional versus moral treatment" divide. Hincks hailed from Ontario and had himself experienced bouts of depression. A sickly but highly precocious child, he attended the University of Toronto at fifteen and graduated in 1907 as a physician at the age of twenty-two. After several years, in which he attempted to establish himself as a professor and general practitioner, Hincks, influenced by the preeminent Toronto psychiatrist Dr. C. K. Clarke, decided to dedicate his life to the prevention and treatment of mental illness. His plan was four-fold: to assess and reorganize asylums toward progressive moral treatments, to introduce training in mental hygiene (early intervention and promotion of mental health), to encourage research into mental hygiene and treatment, and to screen as widely as possible both citizens and immigrants for mental health concerns. Inspired by Clarke and his friendship with American mental health advocate Clifford Beers, author of *A Mind that Found Itself* (an autobiographical account of Beers' survival of his "treatment" in a brutal asylum, and his eventual recovery), Hincks eventually gained the patronage of the then Governor General of Canada, the Duke of Devonshire, and sufficient financial support from other distinguished Canadians to form the National Committee for Mental Hygiene, and begin its operations.

One of the first tasks of the Committee was to conduct inspections of Canadian asylums. In his assessment of conditions in the institutions at Selkirk and Brandon, Hincks stated that these places were "totally unfit to meet the modern demands of a hospital for the insane," and placed much of the blame on a lack of adequate equipment, resources and training. Hincks' survey of the Alberta asylums was conducted in 1921. On the basis of his study, Hincks railed against what he regarded as overly harsh institutional treatment of the mentally ill, and made a wide range of suggestions for improving conditions at Ponoka, noting that mental patients were "mad, not bad." Unfortunately, governments often move slowly when high costs and significant reforms are required.

• • •

Dr. E. H. Cooke, the new Medical Superintendent, could hardly have been more different from the friendly and charismatic Dr. Dawson, in both personality and perspective. Born in England and educated at Durham University, Cooke was a firm believer in patient discipline, which he regarded as the royal road to cure: "Obedience will give them everything they desire." His goal for Ponoka was to make it run smoothly and efficiently. His style was authoritative, and his instructions were crisp and precise. His forte was bureaucratic (statistical tables and detailed annual reports), which pleased the Government very much. Hospital staff were instructed that, in addition to general discipline, punishment was to be given freely. Cooke also encouraged patient learning about personal flaws and weaknesses, which he encouraged staff to point out at every opportunity.

Under Cooke, the Hospital took on a formal, authoritarian manner. Nurses and male attendants were prohibited from taking meals together. In keeping with the Provincial decision to designate the Ponoka Asylum as a large and efficiently run institution, most patient treatment was not oriented to rehabilitation, but to institutional or custodial care and control. Staff (consisting of physicians, psychiatrists, nurses and both male and female attendants) enforced daily schedules and routines with little variation. The mix of treatments offered to patients was consistent with the requirement of their acceptance and following of these daily plans and consisted of punishment for not doing so, including the use of straitjackets, bed cages, restraint cuffs, wrist and leg shackles, and seclusion in side-rooms constructed along the perimeters of many wards (for purposes of moral regulation). Long gone were the days of no restraints and enclosures.

Hydrotherapy now took a variety of forms, some quite removed from Dawson's idea that a warm, comfortable bath could have a calming effect. Dawson's preferred mode of hydrotherapeutic treatment had involved a "continuous warm bath" achieved by lowering the patient into a deep tub of continuously flowing water of 92-95 degrees Fahrenheit in a dark room for one or two hours a day, during which all vital signs were monitored. Another form of hydrotherapy, which became increasingly common under Cooke's system, involved wrapping patients in cold wet sheets with their arms pinned to their sides. The intensive application of coldness to the entire body purportedly caused a "comparative anemia of the brain which led to relaxation and sleep" and was employed when patients became restless and agitated in ways that were viewed as dysfunctional by Cooke and his staff. Once again, dim lighting and the sound of running water attended the dozing or sleeping patient.

On occasion, baths were prolonged for many hours or even days, with patients sometimes strapped into them and allowed to escape only to use toilets. Sometimes body temperatures were manipulated by putting patients in electric blankets or "heat boxes" (wooden crates with hot bulbs with a head hole to the outside, also referred to as "electric cabinets") and/or alternatively wrapping them in hot or cold blankets to sweat and shiver away their madness. A foul-tasting liquid, paraldehyde, also was used to calm patients or drug them to sleep for short times when hydrotherapy or other temperature treatments alone did not occasion drowsiness. At times, high-pressure jets were employed. Such treatments could readily be turned into tools for punishment. In general, hydrotherapy and related treatments could now be categorized as somewhere between beneficent and vile, depending on their duration, intensity and mode of administration.

In many ways, the treatments offered and forced on patients supported the patient work required to keep the Hospital on a sustainable footing. "Water and work," one of Cooke's mottos, frequently saw patients encouraged to participate in farming, laundering, sewing and mending, food preparation and other essential activities, with the promise of a soothing or not so soothing bath contingent on their acquiescence and productivity. A kind of dual-description of such treatments emerged that summarized them as efforts to simulate normal life and to keep patients healthy and engaged in productive routines, while also enabling more basic and base Hospital-centred motivations in terms of institutional needs. There was little talk of helping patients to acquire what many now refer to as "life skills" that would help them to re-enter society outside the Hospital.

Eight to twelve-hour workdays were normal and rewarded by packs of tobacco, if patients were male. Domestic work performed by female patients was not rewarded because women "should not smoke," and the chores assigned to them would have been parts of their everyday lives in or outside the Hospital. Finally in 1922, occupational therapy was formalized and a single occupational therapist was retained by the Hospital's administration to offer OT to a patient population that then totalled approximately 800 patients. The task of the new OT specialist was primarily to relax the patients and to improve their morale.

• • •

During the 1920s, the expansion of the Hospital's physical plant continued at a rapid pace and included a new nurses' residence, a pathology lab, a room for X-rays, a dental office, a tailor shop, six more residences for staff, as well as a staff garage and recreation hall, four new residences for male patients (including Mayfair-Crescent Heights and Elmcrest-Hillcrest), a recreation centre, and on the farm: a second silo and root house, a bunk house, a dormitory for patients, a new water tower (the reservoir) and a creamery. The new water tower was constructed in 1926 to help curb the danger of fire after the farm's dairy barns and one of its silos had been damaged earlier that year. Like many large farms in the surrounding central Alberta countryside, the Hospital cured its own bacon and ham and made its own butter (at a rate of almost one hundred pounds a week). It also had its own teams of oxen for hauling essential supplies such as coal and lumber. So efficient and productive were the Hospital's physical plant and agricultural arrangements that it was able to sell excess energy and produce to the town of Ponoka. The Hospital laundry handled nearly 15,000 articles of clothing each week. In the early twenties, the Canadian Pacific Railroad built a spur line to the Hospital, making the import of coal and building materials more convenient. There could be little doubt about Dr. Cooke's ability to get things done and his ambition to establish the reputation of his Hospital, the operations of which increasingly reflected his own personality.

• • •

From its founding to the end of the 1920s, the Hospital's patient population not only grew but became much more diversified than had been envisioned by the Alberta Government in 1907. Originally intended to house a rather small number of patients who were considered unable to function sufficiently well in society to ensure their own and others' safety, the Hospital quickly became a destination for those unable to care for themselves for a wide variety of reasons. These included the elderly, unwanted children (often from large and poor families of rural settlers), so-called "prairie women" (who "broke down" from the isolation, toil and the experience of being chattel in a settler life that promised little else), "irresponsible girls" (pregnant teens admitted under the Juvenile Delinquency Act) and the poor and destitute who sought food and shelter in addition to medical treatment. The numbers of this last group grew significantly with an amendment to the Insanity Act in 1924 that allowed voluntary admission. (Those addicted to alcohol and drugs were not admissible until 1936, when an amendment to the Mental Diseases Act allowed them to be patients.) The Hospital's patient population also experienced a temporary increase in 1917 when returning veterans from World War I were admitted for treatment. However, soon thereafter, most of these ex-soldiers were transferred to the Hospital for Returned Soldiers in Red Deer. There was, despite a general recognition of combat-induced "shell shock," little understanding of what now is commonly referred to as post-traumatic stress and its wide range of effects.

In some ways, the treatment regimen offered at Ponoka during the 1920s can be understood as an institutional response to Hospital overcrowding, a phenomenon that would continue and mushroom during the 1930s. By January 1, 1930, the Hospital that originally had been built to accommodate 150 patients was housing 1,086. Recovery rates provided in the annual reports prepared by the Hospital's Superintendent had dropped from a third of all patients admitted in the early 1920s to a quarter of those admitted by the end of the 1920s. Undoubtedly this reflected an increase in the numbers of difficult and severely disturbed patients, especially schizophrenics. However, an ever increasing patient to staff ratio, overcrowding on the wards, a general absence of adequate recreational and leisure activity facilities for patients, and the almost complete absence of training facilities near the Hospital, or for that matter anywhere in the Province, to prepare caregivers for mental health service delivery all contributed to an escalation in patient punishment and forced labour as "treatment," and to a general absence of active attempts to rehabilitate patients for life outside the Hospital.

And yet, treatment of patients in the AHP generally avoided the more severe forms of physical intervention that constituted common practices of general physicians outside the Hospital, when confronted by patients exhibiting mental disorders. These included bloodletting, chemical purgatives, emetics and heavy doses of sedatives and sleeping powders. It was not unusual for patients to show up at the early asylums barely alive from massive loss of blood and other essential body fluids due to such procedures, only to die a short while later. Also, compared to the handling of those suffering from mental disorders who had been placed in prisons, a common occurrence prior to, and even during the asylum age, patient treatment at Ponoka and other North American asylums generally avoided the premeditated, willful administration of harsher forms of punishment.

• • •

Nonetheless, a dramatically sad event in 1928 put in motion proposals to do more to safeguard patients' health, both mentally and physically. On September 15, 1928, patient Dr. Arthur Hobbs, a veterinarian with the Royal Canadian Mounted Police who had been kicked in the head by a horse and suffered from delusions and depression, was placed in a straightjacket and beaten by attendant Walter Scott. Hobbs died shortly thereafter. Because Hobbs believed he was being poisoned, he had refused food that Scott and a new, untrained attendant, Russell Lord, had served him. Hobbs' passive refusal to eat enraged Scott who began to beat Hobbs about his chest and face. After placing Hobbs in a straightjacket, Scott continued to beat him in another room. With several broken bones and a punctured lung, Hobbs contracted pneumonia and died. Lord, who had reported Scott's actions to the Medical Superintendent, Dr. Cooke, was attacked by seven fellow attendants, covered by a sheet, beaten and nearly drowned when his head was submerged in a tub of ice-cold water. His attackers were immediately apprehended and each sentenced to two-months in prison. Scott, who continuously maintained his innocence, was tried in the Red Deer Court and sentenced to five years imprisonment.[6] Eventually, he returned to work at the Ponoka Hospital.[7] But things did not stop there. Given the publicity the case enjoyed, many Alberta citizens asked themselves and provincial officials how it was that an ill man who had merely declined to eat could be subjected to such violence.

After Alberta Minister of Health George Hoadley and Alberta Premier John Brownlee refused a Public Inquiry into the matter, government officials (so as to be seen to be doing something in response

---

6   The account of the Hobbs-Lord-Scott incident given here is compiled from reports in Alberta newspapers at the time, together with a recent revisiting of the entire affair published in the *Red Deer Express* on November 30, 2016, under the heading "A Look at the Tragedy of Dr. Arthur Hobbs."

7   Doreen Sturla-Scott (2009). *High Hopes – Degrees of Graduation*. A memoir available on Kindle through Amazon. Sturla-Scott seems to accept Walter Scott's protestations of innocence.

to the Hobbs incident) turned once again to Dr. Hincks and a second progressive psychiatrist, Dr. C. B. Farrar. The Hincks-Farrar report emphasized that the Ponoka Hospital and more recently established, smaller (but ever growing) facilities for the insane at Red Deer and Oliver (on the outskirts of Edmonton) were badly over-crowded, and under and poorly staffed. Specific recommendations concerning the Ponoka Hospital included the reduction of the patient population to no more than 1,000 patients "or preferably to 950 unless further dormitory and day-room space is added," the transfer of patients to other Provincial institutions, and the expansion of existing buildings. In addition, Hincks and Farrar recommended adding two physicians and twenty nurses, to bring staff to patient ratios closer to, but still somewhat higher than, those recommended by the American Psychiatric Association for the staffing of psychiatric institutions. Hincks and Farrar also suggested several ways in which medical staff might be redeployed to "make possible the expenditure of a greater proportion of…time for the direction of clinical work, and for the raising of the level of humanitarian and scientific care of the patients." Several additional recommendations placed further emphasis on the necessity of ensuring that treatments made available for the patients at the Ponoka Hospital be more humane and up-to-date. In particular, Hincks and Farrar strongly objected to the mechanical restraint and seclusion of patients in side-rooms and recommended "the reduction of mechanical constraint with the ultimate aim of its discontinuance," which they stressed would require further "training and augmenting of the nursing staff, and widening the scope of occupational and hydrotherapy." In their discussion of these matters, the two commissioners provided the following historical and humanitarian context:

> A century ago, disturbed patients were chained, manacled and subjected to many types of mechanical restraint. In the last decade of the 18th century, Wm. Tuke of York, England and Philippe Pinel of Paris demonstrated that restraint was

unnecessary in the treatment of restless disturbed mental patients and they advocated its abandonment on both human-itarian and scientific grounds...The use of restraint cannot be justified for rendering restless or mischievous patients less troublesome, preventing destructiveness or other usual expressions of excitement...Usually the most that can be said for restraint is that it renders the patient innocuous, but its use suggests rather a failure of the therapeutic system... At the Ponoka Hospital...this method of control is used to excess and in forms that are unduly severe. The four cage beds should be discontinued; and if it is considered desirable to keep camisoles in reserve for emergencies they should be so constructed as to permit the arms to rest in comfortable positions...The utilization of mechanical restraint reduces the work of nurses and attendants to guard duty that disposes of difficult restless patients by an easy short cut method...If a mental hospital conceives its duty to be the promotion of recovery of patients rather than the convenience of staff, there will be little disposition to use restraint or seclusion. It is an unquestioned fact that restraint instead of quieting a patient tends to make him more rebellious and to increase rather than diminish mental perturbation.[8]

Hincks and Farrar also suggested expansion of therapeutic forms of, and facilities for, beneficent hydrotherapy and occupational therapy as essential to the humanizing of therapeutic practices at Ponoka. In specific reference to the death of Dr. Arthur Hobbs, Hincks and Farrar recommended the Hospital's own policies concerning the general pro-hibition of force-feeding should be taught and followed scrupulously

---

8   *Report of Commissioners Appointed to Investigate the Provincial Training School at Red Deer, Provincial Mental Institute at Oliver, Provincial Mental Hospital at Ponoka,* January 11th, 1929 (Provincial Archives of Alberta).

by all staff and that staff, especially male attendants, be better educated and selected for their duties at the Hospital.

• • •

Unfortunately, about one month after Hincks and Farrar submitted their report to the Alberta Provincial Government, another death occurred at the Ponoka Hospital, which pointed directly to the need for more staff and patient accommodation. In this instance, patient James Walsh was punched violently in the nose by fellow patient William McCausland and died from his injuries several days later, on February 9th, 1929. The jury that considered the case, including evidence presented by coroner Dr. H. S. Vange, concluded that more facilities for patient accommodation would have allowed for the segregation of different types of patients and conceivably might have prevented the tragedy.[9]

On receiving and subsequently considering the extensive findings and recommendations of Hincks and Farrar, the Alberta Government accepted the report and promised to take appropriate action. However, as will become obvious in the next chapter, little changed, despite Cooke's eventual resignation as Medical Superintendent at Ponoka. Subsequent superintendents held a more humane view of patient treatment and care, and did attempt to eliminate restraint and the more controversial versions of hydrotherapy and related body temperature therapies. But, overcrowding continued to be a major problem for many years, due in no small measure to the severe financial constraints and the difficult life circumstances of many Albertans during the "dirty thirties" on the Canadian prairies.

The Hobbs murder and the death of James Walsh also shone a much-needed light on one of the most pressing problems concerning staffing at Ponoka and other asylums: the woefully inadequate training

---

9   "Report on James Walsh, Deceased," Sessional Paper No. 33, Alberta Legislative Assembly, 1929 (Provincial Archives of Alberta).

of hospital attendants, or orderlies. Attendants were omnipresent in the lives of asylum patients, yet they undoubtedly constituted the weakest link in the daily treatment of those patients. They were the individuals in most frequent contact with patients, yet had almost no preparation for their jobs. Fortunately, things were about to change. One of the great contributions of the Ponoka Hospital during the early 1930s was the implementation of rigorous and prolonged preparation programs for the education and training of psychiatric nurses and attendants.

• • •

When I try to imagine the lives of patients at Ponoka and other asylums during the first few decades of the twentieth century, I often think of my paternal grandmother. She certainly could have qualified as one of those "prairie women" who, together with their farmer spouses, accounted for at least half of the new admissions to the Ponoka Hospital each year in the 1920s (according to the meticulously compiled tables in Superintendent Cooke's annual reports). After the death of her husband from the post-World War I influenza, my grandmother was left alone to raise eight children on a lonely, dry and flat Southern Alberta farm pretty much in the middle of nowhere. She had no choice but to give over the family farm and its operation to the brother of her deceased husband and allow him to determine the few educational and career opportunities available to her sons, who as soon as they could manage a day's hard work in the fields, were removed from school and accommodated in brother Wilhelm's "large white house," together with his wife and their children. I've visited the house (actually of very modest size when compared to contemporary homes), which has been preserved and moved to the municipal heritage park in the hamlet of Enchant. It is difficult to imagine how as many as fifteen people could possibly have found room to sleep, let alone live, in the place. But, whatever amenities they enjoyed probably exceeded those experienced by my grandmother and her daughters in the original farm house that had once belonged to my great-grandparents. It is not at all difficult to imagine the "prairie woman" in my grandmother. And, it is not surprising to me that by the time I was born in 1950, she had become decidedly fey—extremely religious in a very personal and vocal way and often conversing with the "little people" inside the radio and TV, even as she toiled endlessly to produce crocheted doily after crocheted doily.

By the late 1950s, my grandmother couldn't be left to live alone. She stayed for a while with us, and then with various others of my uncles, aunts and cousins, usually moving when her constant—mostly but not always—false accusations about the maleficence of us children had become unbearable. I recall one instance in which she accused me of stealing what in those days was the significant amount of five dollars, a bill she apparently had tucked into the well-thumbed bible that she carried with her most of the day. What was most painful and upsetting was not the accusation, but the anguished look of intense disappointment she directed at me as she made her allegation.

Given that not only my father and mother, but two of my father's sisters, lived in Ponoka, and both my father and one sister worked at the Hospital, it was natural, but far from easy, for them to have my grandmother assessed and committed there, after which she was quickly moved to the Provincial Auxiliary Hospital in Claresholm, Alberta. The hospital at Claresholm was opened in 1933 in what had been the Claresholm School of Agriculture. It was home to many older female patients by the time my grandmother lived there. I very much hope, but have no way of knowing for sure, despite my occasional but increasingly infrequent visits, that she was treated well. Like many of those for whom Hincks advocated so eloquently, she had become a very difficult person, but never was a bad one.

CHAPTER TWO:
DEPRESSION

I was researching a high school essay about the Middle Ages when I first came across the practice of trepanning—boring or scraping into the human skull so as to allow evil spirits to exit the head, and thus cure abnormal behaviour or madness. Practiced in many historical cultures, and with a few stubbornly clinging adherents to this day, it qualifies as a physically invasive version of exorcism, which, accompanied by purging and bloodletting, was frequently used in pre-asylum treatments of mental illness provided by clergy and others. The idea that mental illness can be alleviated by surgical and other forms of physical intervention has a very long history, dating at least to the ancient Greeks. The modern history of psychiatry is in many ways a story concerning a surprisingly varied set of either biophysical or interpersonal social psychological approaches to the treatment of mental illness. The social, humane and educational methods of moral treatment advocated by some in the late 1800s and early 1900s, and in contemporary psychotherapy, exemplify the social psychological approaches; trepanning and its modern variants like lobotomy and electroshock therapy, now referred to as electroconvulsive therapy (ECT), exemplify the biophysical approaches. Also on the biophysical side of the treatment dimension are a host of other interventions, some of which form an important part of the history of the Alberta Hospital Ponoka.

• • •

When I first read the annual reports prepared by the various Medical Superintendents of the Ponoka Hospital,[10] I was puzzled by the recurring phrase "malarial treatment." It was described in Superintendent Cooke's annual report for 1924 as a method "of treating General Paralysis, which hitherto has proved one of the most fatal of maladies...by inoculation with the malarial parasite, of which a benign strain (plasmodium vivax) was obtained from the University Hospital [presumably the University of Alberta Hospital in Edmonton that was established in 1906]. In fourteen cases placed under treatment, the results have been encouraging and justify a more extended trial." So what was all this about?

Among the patients at Ponoka were a number of individuals suffering from mental illness caused by late-stage syphilis, in several cases contracted during the "Great War." Most of those in early stages of the disease lived relatively normal lives. However, more advanced cases admitted to the Hospital suffered from bizarre beliefs, terrifying visions and general paresis. On visiting Bedlam in London, England (more formally, Bethlem Royal Hospital), Cooke became familiar with a new treatment for general paresis—general paralysis—a condition caused by tertiary syphilis affecting the brain, which is characterized by a wide variety of psychological dysfunction and disturbance, and by weakened muscles, so that patients have great difficulty moving

---

10   In addition to the secondary sources cited in Chapter One, the annual reports of the medical superintendent of the Ponoka Hospital from 1930 to 1939 constitute the main primary sources for the material contained in this chapter. Additional secondary sources concerning the history of psychiatry and psychiatric treatments are drawn from a variety of books and articles, and from my own notes and lectures compiled over many years of teaching the history of psychology at Simon Fraser University. Primary sources other than the annual reports are footnoted separately.

arms, legs and other parts of the body; they also experience seizures. The treatment had been developed by Austrian physician, Dr. Julius Wagner-Jauregg, whose life's work was devoted to the treatment of mental illness through inducing fever—a general approach called pyrotherapy. In 1917, Wagner-Jauregg had treated general paresis by injecting the least aggressive malaria parasite, plasmodium vivax, to produce high and prolonged fevers, which hopefully could be treated, if necessary, by quinine. For this work, Wagner-Jauregg was awarded the Nobel Prize in Medicine in 1927. Wagner-Jauregg went on to treat schizophrenia (thought to be caused by excessive masturbation) with sterilization, and to administer thyroid and ovarian preparations to psychotic patients whose puberty was delayed in an attempt to encourage the development of secondary sexual characteristics and reduce their psychoses. He was also an anti-Semite, and later became a member of the Nazi Party and an advocate for eugenics.

On his return to Ponoka, Cooke first used the malarial method to treat patient Eldon Snipps, who was still in the early stages of syphilis. Three days following the injection, Snipps was shivering from chills severe enough for hospital staff to wrap him and put him in a side room. Shortly thereafter he began to sweat profusely. After twelve hours of swapping chills and fever, Cooke injected Snipps with quinine, apparently leading to his recovery with an improved mental and physical condition. Throughout the rest of the 1920s, malarial treatment continued to be given at the Ponoka Hospital to both patients committed to the institution and those who voluntarily admitted themselves, many of the latter specifically seeking treatment for early stages of syphilis. Unfortunately, from tables listing the causes of patient deaths at the Hospital (contained in the annual reports), it is clear that not all cases of malarial treatment were successful, and that some patient deaths (for example, two in 1927 and two in 1929) were directly attributable to the procedure. Cooke's overall success rate in treating syphilitics with malaria therapy was about sixty per cent. During his final years at the Hospital, Cooke made use of "carrier patients," who were infected with the malaria parasite, to transfer, by blood, the virus to other patients undergoing active treatment. Even after Cooke resigned as Superintendent on August 31, 1931, the Hospital at Ponoka continued to treat sixty to eighty cases of syphilis each year, mostly voluntary admissions. However, by 1934, a wider range of treatments, some less potentially dangerous than malarial therapy, was employed, and almost no deaths related directly to these treatments were recorded. When penicillin became readily available to treat syphilis in its early stages, malarial therapy was gradually retired. Nonetheless, a few advanced cases continued to be treated at the Hospital, and "carrier patients" were maintained and used into the 1950s. The following passage from psychiatric nurse Doreen Sturla-Scott's memoir of her experiences at the Hospital[11] describes a typical instance of malarial treatment.

> ...two "carrier" patients were maintained at the hospital, with the malarial bug forever within their systems...and who had had the malarial treatment...The treatment was brutal. For days, the fever produced by injecting blood from the carrier patient was allowed to rage in the person, and finally, after three weeks to a month of this fever, anti-fever medication was prescribed, and the person was determined to be free of syphilis. Sometimes it worked, sometimes it did not, but this was before the prescribing of penicillin, and most persons felt it was a chance to avoid the crippling and most debilitating effects of the paresis. (pp. 2-3, Chapter Five)

• • •

When Cooke resigned, he was replaced temporarily as Superintendent by Dr. Charles Arthur Baragar who, in the previous year, had been appointed Provincial Commissioner of Mental Institutions, and

---

11   Doreen Sturla-Scott (2009). *High Hopes – Degrees of Graduation*. Available from Amazon on Kindle.

Director of Mental Health. Before coming to Alberta, Baragar, born in Ontario and educated at the University of Manitoba, had been Medical Superintendent at Brandon, where he had modernized that institution and established a proper training program for psychiatric nurses, but he had clashed with union leaders who represented many of his medical staff. Baragar was considered one of the most progressive psychiatrists in Canada. Well aware of the report of Hincks and Farrar, he was anxious that the new permanent Superintendent at Ponoka be cut from a different cloth than Cooke. However, he also found himself and his portfolio stressed for funds as the "dirty thirties" descended on Western Canada. Given these circumstances, Baragar inserted himself as Acting Medical Superintendent of the AHP so that he could take the time to find an appropriate permanent superintendent, while simultaneously taking a prolonged, first-hand look at the Hospital's operations and practices. By all accounts, his accomplishments during the seven months he oversaw Hospital operations directly (August 15, 1931 to March 15, 1932) were remarkable.

During this time, Baragar, indefatigable in his roles as Superintendent of Ponoka and Commissioner of all the Province's mental health facilities and programs, completely reorganized the Department of Mental Diseases and Mental Institutions to support a more modern and progressive approach to mental health services and their delivery. At Ponoka, he reorganized staff conferences "with a view to having all new cases thoroughly worked up and presented to the medical staff as a group as soon after admission as practicable." He also reorganized the ward arrangement "so as to permit of greater classification of patients on admission, for the assembling of physically ill patients in special infirmary wards, and for the more effective classification of all patients on the chronic wards of the hospital. To facilitate the work of the medical officers and to stress the importance of their clinical work and their responsibility for direction and control of treatment, their offices were decentralized." Whereas these offices formally were grouped together in the administration section of the Hospital, they now were moved onto the wards themselves in close proximity to the patients and ward staff.

Baragar, in collaboration with Dr. Harold Orr and the Province's Social Hygiene Division, also streamlined and attempted to safeguard as much as possible "malarial treatment as a prophylactic measure in cases of early neurosyphilis," returning those treated as quickly as possible to smaller provincial clinics for the duration of their treatment—a small but significant step to mitigate the overcrowding that was now chronic in the Ponoka facility. Many of Baragar's initiatives were informed by, and consistent with, the numerous recommendations made to the Provincial Government of Alberta by Hincks and Farrar in 1928.

Baragar's concern for patients and his general philosophy of their care and treatment were reflected clearly in his end-of-year, annual report for 1931. In discussing occupational therapy in the form of patient work at the Hospital, Baragar commented that:

> Properly applied under competent psychiatric and technical direction, it is the most important single therapeutic agent we have outside the influence of personal contacts and relationships. It must be remembered, however, that industrial occupation is a two-edged weapon. The intentional or unintentional injection of an element of exploitation might do much harm. It is important, therefore, that the objectives of both personal and direct institutional benefit be kept prominently in mind in all occupational activities.

In light of Baragar's remarks, it is important to note that occupational therapy and other attempts to involve patients in work and life pursuits (including games, sports, entertainments, festivities, day passes or leaves, and other outings) are often mentioned in various asylum histories as having great benefits for both patients and members of the public. Exposure to the patients in normal settings helped the wider communities to gain a better and first-hand understanding of those suffering from mental disorders, potentially cutting through prevalent stereotypes, and encouraging patients to conduct themselves in generally more "normal" ways. Many hospital superintendents at institutions like Ponoka have commented on the apparent fact that when placed in everyday social settings (e.g., playing cards or watching cinema), the behaviour of many asylum patients was surprisingly "appropriate" and "normal." Wisconsin Hospital Superintendent Adin Sherman, in 1918, remarked that when viewing motion pictures, "The patients are highly entertained and show great appreciation of the comedies which are popular with the general public, and an amusing incident no more escapes them than it does a sane audience" (p. 111).[12]

• • •

Baragar's continued presence on-site at Ponoka was assured when he formally moved his office as Provincial Commissioner of Mental Institutions and Director of Mental Health to the Ponoka Hospital. Thus, when Baragar's hand-picked successor to the position of Medical Superintendent of the Hospital, Dr. George A. Davidson, settled into his new job on March 16, 1932, Baragar was right there to help him weather some of the worst overcrowding and tightest budgets the Hospital was to experience during the deepest part of the 1930s Depression. Baragar's motivation was not only that Ponoka was the largest psychiatric facility, and therefore had the most effect on the Province's sick, but also that it was closely linked to one of his pet projects, the work of training nurses and attendants at the new educational facility he located at the Ponoka Hospital.

The inauguration of this training facility had been one of Baragar's first acts upon coming to Alberta in the Fall of 1930, and he was determined that nothing should happen to prevent its realization. In his own words, in the 1932 annual report of the Provincial Mental Hospital,

---

12   Quoted in Thomas G. Ebert (1999). *A Social History of the Asylum: Mental Illness and its Treatment in the Late 19th and Early 20th Century.* Bristol, IN: Wyndham Hall Press.

Ponoka: "The importance of this training cannot be over-estimated. The intelligent and sympathetic nursing care of mental patients is dependent on such training even more, if possible, than in general nursing." A small example of such care and concern was his effort to secure more festive clothing for patients able to attend social activities, such as fortnightly dances, so that they might escape from their "stereotyped hospital clothing...and improve the enjoyment for all." It was with great satisfaction that Baragar was able to oversee the first graduation of nurses and attendants from the training school at Ponoka in 1933, when eight nurses and twenty-three attendants received their certificates after successfully completing the three-year program. Baragar also extended himself and his staff of physicians by making all medical officers at the hospital available for conversations with visiting family members of patients, to "engender a spirit of confidence in the work of the hospital, as well as to gain outside information regarding the patient."

• • •

Having worked in a number of different clinical and educational contexts, I cannot overstate the importance of the kind of generally enlightened leadership that Baragar and some other administrators exercised at the Ponoka Hospital. Through my professional and personal experience, I have come to think that there are two broad kinds of administrator—those who tend to enjoy the pomp and status of their roles but give insufficient attention to the people, both staff and clients, for whom they are responsible, and those who tend to put perks aside and energetically direct the authority and resources of their offices to improving the work and life conditions of their employees and clients. I say "tend" because no administrator or anyone else is free of faults and mistakes. Yet, it is quickly apparent to staff and those in receipt of their ministrations whether the people at the top are primarily in it for themselves, or are primarily committed to doing their actual jobs. Of course, this way of seeing things, although I think it is generally accurate, also is subject to debate. As one of my students, a young Oscar Wilde incarnate, remarked after hearing some version of it, "Yes and there also are two other kinds of people: those who think there are two kinds of people and those who don't."

• • •

At any rate, no matter how you cut it, Baragar was mostly a very good thing for the Ponoka Hospital, its patients and its staff, and for mental health services in the Province of Alberta. Unfortunately, Dr. Charles Arthur Baragar died of pneumonia in Edmonton on March 8, 1936, shortly after taking on the duties of Medical Superintendent at Ponoka for a second time on January 1, 1936, following Dr. Davidson's return to private practice in 1935.

Dr. George A. Davidson had worked with Baragar at Brandon. His biggest challenge as Superintendent of the Ponoka Hospital was to cope with the constantly increasing overcrowding of the facility, which eventually reached a peak of 1,707 patients in 1937. In his 1934 report, Davidson wrote: "The most depressing aspect of the whole work is the constant increase in overcrowding with no immediate prospect of relief in any direction." Despite the opening of the Claresholm Auxiliary Hospital in 1933, and the transfer of some patients to the Psychiatric Hospital at Oliver, the Great Depression and general population growth in the Province continued to flood the Provincial Mental Hospital, Ponoka with new admissions throughout the 1930s. No amount of shuffling patients from one crowded institution to another, or re-purposing older facilities like the Claresholm School of Agriculture or the Red Deer Veteran's Hospital, could stand in for the much-needed construction of new facilities. Yet, nothing apparently could be done until the Province's financial situation improved.

• • •

The truth was that the Great Depression was greatest in the Canadian prairies, which were hit by a triple whammy: embargoes and quotas were set by many European countries who were major importers of Canadian wheat, to protect their own farmers following the market crash of 1929; huge increases in worldwide grain shipments from new agricultural exporters like Australia and Argentina led to large surpluses—a bushel of number one Northern dropped from $1.03 in 1928 to 29 cents by 1932 and the average Alberta farm income was cut in half; and dust storms, drought and scorching winds that, by 1936, dried lakes, encouraged swarms of locusts and exploding populations of gophers, and destroyed top soil made tenuous from years of over tilling. Millions of prairie acres literally blew away. No sector of the economy suffered as much or recovered as slowly as the prairie farms in Canada. With federal and provincial governments combatting the ravages of the Dirty 30s, mental health, even as it deteriorated along with conditions on the farms, was almost an afterthought in Provincial funding priorities.[13]

My mother-in-law used to recall how, in the early thirties, the cream she helped her mother deliver for sale to the Ponoka Dairy "one week received a record price, and the next week nothing at all." Many farmers and ranchers were able to subsist on produce from their own labours, often with exchanges of favours and barter with neighbours. At this same time, my own mother and her siblings did much of whatever farming remained to be done as their mother returned to shop work in Hughenden, and their father continued to teach and scavenge materials and supplies for students. But none of this prepared her for the kind of poverty and shortage of supplies that awaited her in Enchant when she arrived to teach there in 1936.

The parkland of Central Alberta supported a more diversified mixed farming which provided somewhat greater quantity and variety to the

---

13   Statistical information reported here is drawn from several sections of the 1985, *Canadian Encyclopedia*. Edmonton, AB: Hurtig Publishers.

self-sustaining diets of rural families than did the arid, flat plains further south. Just outside of Enchant, my father's extensive blended family was able to get through the worst of things as older siblings supplemented the meager yields and profit from their vanishing wheat crop with what some of them earned by working a variety of temporary jobs in surrounding towns, and on larger and better run farming operations. Throughout the rural areas of the Province of Alberta, homemakers collected soap remnants that they tied up into bits of tattered hose to be used for washing, defunct machinery was stripped of any and every reusable bit and part, and paper of any kind found a place in kitchens and outhouses.

For those of us born after the Second World War, our parents' experiences and stories of life during the 1930s provided a never-ending litany of censor and advice of "waste not, want not." When jumpers became popular wear for young girls during the 1960s, my wife's mother hated the fashion for reminding her of the improvised jumpers she and her sisters had been forced to wear in the thirties when sleeves of dresses deteriorated from wear and tear. It took all my wife's teenage guile to secure a jumper that she still remembers with great fondness. My own mother developed a life-long phobia to dirt and mud that seemed to her to be everywhere in her Depression experience, the seasons affecting only the consistency of the unwanted earth. She could be found at regular times each day of her life sweeping away the small amounts of dirt that accumulated on our doorstep and in our entry way, a habit I seem to have acquired from her to the point where a recent birthday gift from my wife was an artisan crafted broom. As I write this, a small grandson who lives nearby has picked up the habit. For many, like my father, the thirties meant loss and the necessity of making a fresh start, a reality that brought him and my mother, who married in 1942, to Ponoka to begin a new life together. For many Alberta baby boomers, like my wife and myself, stories of 1930s hardships imbided during our childhoods served as life-long warnings and reminders that things always could get worse. To this day, my way of coping with almost any eventuality is to imagine what the very worst possibility might be and take sustenance from the fact that we aren't there yet.

• • •

Despite the chronic and increasing overcrowding and Depression-era underfunding that beset George Davidson's time as Medical Superintendent of the Ponoka Hospital, he was able to continue to build on Dr. Baragar's progressive reforms. He increased the rate of genuinely therapeutic occupational therapy (including getting almost all patients outside on a regular basis), improved the surgical facilities at the Hospital, supported and expanded the training program and facilities for nurses and attendants, installed a general library for patients, established a print shop and book bindery, and encouraged more contacts with the families of residents who visited the hospital, and with the Province's Mental Hygiene Clinics. Nonetheless, and perhaps unsurprisingly, by the end of 1935, Dr. Davidson had experienced enough of the stresses of institutional overcrowding and underfunding, and escaped the Prairie Depression to take up a practice in psychiatry in Vancouver.

The 1930s also witnessed a marked increase in operations to sterilize patients at the Alberta Hospital Ponoka and elsewhere in the Alberta mental health system. The Sexual Sterilization Act was passed on March 21, 1928 and authorized the activities of the Eugenics Board of Alberta.[14] The first operation took place on May 10, 1929. By the time Dr. Davidson retired from his position at Ponoka, 395 sterilizations had been performed in Alberta, the majority of them at the Provincial Mental Hospital, Ponoka. What might surprise many readers was that two of the most progressive psychiatrists to serve as

---

14   Much of the information included in this section is informed by the annual reports of the Eugenics Board, Province of Alberta, from 1933 to 1953, and related Provincial Government documents concerning the operation of this Board. These documents are located in the Provincial Archives of Alberta in Edmonton.

medical Superintendents at Ponoka, Dr. Baragar and Dr. Davidson, were members of the Eugenics Board of Alberta from 1930 to 1936, during which time patients undergoing sterilization were required to assent to the procedure. It was not until 1937 that the requirement of patient consent sometimes could be removed for "mentally defective" persons. Consent for those considered mentally ill but not "defective" remained in place until the Alberta Government finally stopped legal sterilization in 1972, one of the last governments in the world to do so.

Prior to the removal of the more restrictive constraint in 1937, fifteen percent of cases considered by the Board were sterilized. Following the 1937 decision to partially remove consent, eighty-nine percent of cases considered resulted in sterilization. In 1942, an amendment to the Mental Defectives Act permitted the discharge of patients from mental facilities such as Ponoka only if they were able to care for themselves, did not pose a threat to others, and had been sexually sterilized. Alberta and British Columbia were the only Canadian Provinces to legalize sterilization. Youth, aboriginals and women were sterilized in disproportionately high numbers. Although making up approximately three percent of the population of Alberta, aboriginals and Métis comprised a quarter of those sterilized.

• • •

Widespread public awareness of forced sterilization in Alberta's history followed the release of the documentary film, *The Sterilization of Leilani Muir*, in 1996. Leilani Muir, an unwanted and abused child, was admitted to the Provincial Training School for Mental Defectives in Red Deer Alberta in 1955, at age ten, on the basis of information provided by her mother, who also signed a form permitting legal sterilization of her daughter. The mother's signature on the form was a precondition to the facility's acceptance of Leilani, who thought she was being placed in an orphanage. Administered an IQ test prior to being interviewed by the Eugenics Board, Leilani recorded a score of 64, placing her in the category of Mental Defective Moron, sufficient basis for her sterilization under the operating rules of the Board. She was told that she was undergoing an appendectomy, but Leilani's fallopian tubes were made dysfunctional during the operation. Only a decade later, after release from the Training School at the age of twenty, did she discover that she could not bear children. Recovering from her ordeals and living in British Columbia, Muir subsequently scored 89 on an IQ test. She then sued the Alberta Government and was awarded $740,780 in damages and $230,000 for legal fees. In the judgment of Alberta Justice Joanne B. Veit: "because the government's own standards for sterilization were ignored in Ms. Muir's case, the conduct of the government was more than negligent, it was intentional. The sterilization became an assault and battery." Justice Veit also found the government responsible for Ms. Muir's loss of privacy and liberty, and the imposition of institutional discipline, and the unwarranted administration of antipsychotic drugs.[15]

> Ms. Muir was made to diaper adult "inmates" who had lost control of their bowel functions, and she was made to eat mush with a spoon. She was sent to wards with straight-jacketed inmates where she scrubbed floors...slept in a small cement room, with a rubber mattress and ate out of a tin bowl...many anti-psychotic drugs were administered to Ms. Muir despite the fact that she was not psychotic. Indeed, it appears from his publications in professional journals that [hospital psychiatrist] Dr. le Van used Ms. Muir and others as a means of testing the success of different drug treatments.

The Alberta Government eventually apologized for the forced sterilization of over 2,800 Albertans, and paid 140 million dollars in damages. Muir herself eventually made her home in Devon, Alberta among friends and family, and continued to speak and write about her experiences. The play, *Leilani Muir and the Alberta Eugenics Board,* was performed at the 2012 Edmonton Fringe Festival.

---

15   Muir v. The Queen in right of Alberta 132 D. L. R. (4th) 695. Court File No. 8903 20759.

Much has been written about eugenics movements and sterilization, voluntary and involuntary, so many Albertans and Canadians are familiar with this episode in mental health "treatment." However, it may be very difficult for many reading this text to understand the general attitude of the public in the 1930s to sterilization, especially forced sterilization. At the time, the vast majority of Canadians, Americans and citizens of many other countries believed that such procedures were warranted—at best as ways of ensuring that vulnerable infants would not be born to those without the ability and means to support and care for them; at worst as a way of guarding against the degeneration of the human race. Both rationales were voiced by Alberta politicians William Aberhart and Ernest Manning, and women's rights activists like Nellie McClung and Emily Murphy, who also argued that children born to mental patients were more likely to be born handicapped and be a drain on the public purse.

• • •

I believe another perspective worth considering when thinking about sterilization at this time is that of parents of developmentally challenged children who cared deeply about their children and provided them with as much love and support as they could for as long as they could, yet who also were anxious that their children be sterilized and gave their informed consent to the procedure. When I was ten years old, a cousin of my mother's and his wife, who were very close friends of my parents, welcomed a new baby into their lives, an infant who was born with Down's Syndrome. Over the next fifteen years, I watched the child grow and flourish under the love and care provided by her parents and older brother, doing much better and living longer than the family was led to believe would be possible by the physicians and other experts they consulted and worked with. Unfortunately, when her mother died, the young woman became depressed and inconsolable for a long period of time, and given her deteriorating mental and physical health, the family eventually placed her in a mental health facility, where she maintained her condition but never improved. During my last visit with her dying mother, a lapsed but not inattentive Catholic, she told me the decision to sterilize her daughter was hers and hers alone, and that it was the most difficult thing she ever had done, and also the thing that was most in her mind during her dying. As far as I could gather, and as far as she herself knew, her reasons were not about anything other than ensuring that her daughter would enjoy the best life possible, a life within which she was able to cope and flourish as much as the challenges she faced allowed. None of this is intended to condone involuntary sterilization as practiced in Alberta and British Columbia at provincial psychiatric facilities in the past. Rather, it is an attempt to capture another perspective that belonged to this particular historical period and might not be immediately available to some readers. As my Wildean student implied, sometimes there are many perspectives on a difficult matter that deserve consideration.

• • •

Following Davidson's departure for the coast and Baragar's death, Dr. Randall Roberts MacLean was appointed acting Superintendent of the Ponoka Hospital, and after proving himself well up to the job, soon advanced to the Superintendency itself. MacLean was born in Newcastle, New Brunswick in 1900, graduated as a licensed teacher from the New Brunswick Normal School in 1918 and came West to teach in Saskatchewan. Shortly thereafter, he was admitted as part of the first cohort to enter a new six-year MD program at the University of Alberta, from which he graduated in May, 1927. After a year interning at the University of Alberta Hospital, he moved south and worked at the Ponoka Hospital from late 1927 to 1929 before obtaining a leave of absence during which he studied psychiatry firsthand, as practiced in Boston, London and Zurich. When he took over as Acting Superintendent in 1936, MacLean was anxious to implement a wide variety of progressive treatments, but found that he had his hands full dealing with massive overcrowding, aging buildings and insufficient funds to hire additional staff and undertake new initiatives.

By the start of 1936, the patient population at the Ponoka Hospital had swelled to 1,490. It peaked at 1,707 during 1937. In his 1936 annual report, MacLean noted that there was "Great concern...for the safety of a large number of defenseless patients on the overcrowded wards. In some instances, there is scarcely enough room for the patients to sit about comfortably, and when moving about, there is great liability to being pushed or attacked as a result of coming into physical contact with others." The danger that MacLean was addressing here was clearly a result of overcrowding, but also was exacerbated by the kinds of admission the overcrowding had created. Given that overcrowding now had been ongoing for a number of years, only those patients most requiring incarceration were being admitted. Less difficult cases were actively being channeled to the Province's Mental Hygiene Clinics or, on occasion, being dealt with in the Province's general hospitals. Increasingly, those with drug and alcohol addictions were refused admission, on the basis that "In most instances these individuals had been here before, and it was thought that very few were helped materially by treatment." Even so, the still high rate of new admissions and increasing ratios of patients to staff members meant that assessment of and attention to individual patients' needs were being compromised. In addition, not only had no new accommodation been constructed for several years, but the available buildings were deteriorating rapidly due to a shortage of funds for ongoing maintenance. Many patients were being housed in hallways and make-shift dormitories in which temperatures fluctuated greatly and dampness was common.

Under such conditions, it is perhaps not surprising that there were outbreaks of influenza in 1936 and 1937, and acute infective enterocolitis in 1937. In 1936, thirty-seven deaths resulted from pneumonia precipitated by the influenza. In 1937, eleven deaths were directly attributed to influenza, and ten, directly to acute enterocolitis. Most of these deaths were amongst elderly patients. In both 1936 and

1937, a high number of patient injuries inflicted by other patients were reported and in 1937, a staff member was "badly beaten about the head by a patient, sustaining multiple skull fractures to which he subsequently succumbed."[16]

The overcrowding at the Hospital finally was addressed a bit when, in 1938, eleven female patients were transferred to Claresholm, and more so in 1939, when 121 women were transferred to Claresholm and the newly opened Raymond Auxiliary Hospital (located in what had been the Raymond Agricultural Centre), and twenty male patients were transferred to the Edmonton Provincial Mental Institute at Oliver. Although the male patients were considered refractory (difficult to manage), all the female patients transferred were "of the quiet and elderly types and the transfer served to bring about greater concentrations of refractory women on the female wards." In his annual report of 1939, MacLean summarized the situation that remained after the transfers:

> It is still most imperative that some steps be taken to provide accommodation for the surplus refractory wards on this institution. This overcrowding, which has been the major problem of the institution for years, has created a most difficult situation in the supervision and treatment of these cases, which has been very discouraging to members of the medical and nursing staffs.

• • •

By the end of the 1930s, the patient population at the Hospital had been reduced to 1,557 but had shifted to a larger number of refractory cases. Overcrowding, even if slightly reduced, continued to be a problem, especially on the female refractory wards. Nonetheless, as the

---

16   All quotations in this section are from the annual reports of the Medical Superintendent for the year being discussed.

depression era ended, Dr. MacLean had proved himself to be an effective advocate for what little resources were available. Perhaps most surprisingly, and despite the increase in more difficult cases, he had begun a series of progressive reforms in patient care that included the removal of physical restraints from 1936 onward. It is considerable testimony to MacLean's leadership and humane vision that at the height of hospital overcrowding and declining staff morale, he was able to initiate such a progressive reform. He also ensured a continuation of only the most effective and least punitive forms of hydrotherapy, and an expansion of occupational therapy and therapeutic sites to allow more outdoor activities for patients.

Modest expansion of the Hospital's physical facilities included two new male wards (then called the Rundle-Apollo block and Greencourt) as well as a new Carpentry Shop and a Chicken Ranch and Cannery, all of which contributed to keeping the Hospital on a mostly self-sustaining footing. The patients' library was expanded during the final years of the 1930s. In addition, MacLean placed considerable importance on social, cultural and sporting activities for both staff and patients, with new tennis courts, glee and drama clubs, and improvements to the ice skating and football (soccer) facilities. Like many large psychiatric hospitals at that time, the grounds of the Hospital were well planted and manicured, giving the entire place the appearance of a rather lavish, if somewhat faded, country club, at least from the outside.

Turning to psychiatric education and research, MacLean continued Baragar's and Davidson's strong support for the training programs for psychiatric nurses and attendants, and wanted to conduct and encourage more research at the Hospital, especially related to some of the new treatments he had been exposed to during his postgraduate studies and observations in Boston and in Europe. In almost all of the annual reports he submitted in the late 1930s, he lamented the relative absence of psychiatric research at the hospital. Nonetheless, in addition to trying out some newly developed drug preparations, MacLean and his medical staff did begin to treat a small number of patients with insulin and metrazol shock treatments in 1937, which by the end of 1939, he viewed as promising, opining that "the best results might be expected in the early cases." Together with the ongoing malarial treatments and sterilizations being performed at the hospital, experimentation with such physically invasive "therapies" seems to conflict rather dramatically with the many humane initiatives pursued by MacLean during his tenure as Medical Superintendent at Ponoka. That MacLean himself apparently did not recognize any conflict or inconsistency seems to speak loudly to the zeitgeist of faith in a possible biophysical cure for mental illness that prevailed in much of the psychiatric community at this time.

· · ·

By the late 1930s, psychiatry had intensified its search for more effective medical intervention in the treatment of mental illness. As effective in many cases as occupational therapy, moral therapy and humane hydrotherapy had proven to be, none of these forms of intervention qualified in the minds of most medical practitioners and researchers as "medical" in any real sense that would elevate the scientific reputation of psychiatry as a medical specialty, and the status of psychiatrists as scientists and scientific practitioners. As noted at the beginning of this chapter, physically invasive treatments of the mentally ill date from the middle ages when trepanning of the skull was thought by some to bring order to cerebral chaos. Physical assault of the mentally ill continued throughout much of human history in the form of routine cruelties dished out by societies in fear and disgust at the mentally defective amongst them, and by wardens and custodians of jails, poorhouses, workhouses and early asylums. However, it was not until the 1800s that physically invasive psychiatric procedures began in earnest as legitimate and purposeful attempts to cure the mentally ill. If physical interventions (such as inoculations for an increasing number of diseases from cholera to the plague, a growing number of effective anesthetics, and new inventions including X-rays and aspirin) were possible in general medicine, surely there must exist physical interventions for the diagnosis and treatment of mental illness as well.

By the late 1800s, previously employed physical treatments for the mentally ill (including purging, bloodletting, blistering and dousing patients in either near boiling or near freezing water) had mostly been swept away. Reformers like Dorothy Dix championed the humanitarian paths laid out earlier by Phillipe Pinel in France and William Tuke in the United States. Nonetheless, new quasi or pseudo-scientific proposals for physical interventions continued to arise, such as the "animal magnetism" of Austrian physician Franz Mesmer. Mesmer's cure required several patients, mostly hysterics with symptoms of physical malfunction for which there seemed to be no known physical cause, to be seated around a tub containing chemicals so that iron rods attached to the tub could be applied to their afflicted body parts. Mesmer, dressed in a purple robe, would move from one patient to another, touching them with his hand or a wand. Despite reported success, mesmerism was debunked by Benjamin Franklin on a visit to Paris, and Mesmer's reported successes were attributed to a form of hypnotism.

Depression conditions and overcrowding of asylums during the 1930s cried out for increased rates of cure—the ideal form of which would consist of a decisive physical intervention that would rid patients of their malaise once and for all. To this end, alternative forms of "shock" therapy, whose advocates clung stubbornly to the idea that salubrious effects might attend a "good shock to the patient's physical system," continued to be employed. Introduced in 1927, but not attempted at Ponoka until 1936, insulin shock treatment and metrazol shock treatment were two such physical interventions, used predominately for the treatment of schizophrenia.

• • •

In insulin shock therapy, developed by Austrian psychiatrist Manfred Sakel, patients were injected repeatedly with large doses of insulin that put them in daily comas over several weeks, typically six days a week for about two months. Over the course of forty to fifty comas, the rate of comas was gradually reduced until treatment stopped. Each coma would last for up to an hour, with the patient convulsing during the coma. Between treatments, patients required constant care to guard against hypoglycemic aftershocks. Often patients emerged from the overall treatment being grossly obese. In rare cases, they suffered brain damage and death.

In her memoir, *High Hopes – Degrees of Graduation*,[17] psychiatric nurse Doreen Sturla-Scott describes how insulin coma therapy continued to be used at Ponoka during the 1950s in a more multi-faceted treatment program administered by Dr. Margaret McWilliam, described by Sturla-Scott as a person with "a strong sense of social justice [who] felt deeply the pain her patients felt in their mental illness" (pp. 4-5, Chap. 6). Dr. McWilliam had developed her own theory concerning insulin shock therapy, which she combined with dream-work and group psychotherapy.

> Twelve patients were selected, six men and six women, after a careful study of their problems. Dr. McWilliam believed that when a person was put into a diabetic coma, they would dream their problems, and within the dreaming, find solutions. The program ran from Monday to Friday, with two psychiatric nurses, one male, one female. They would come to work at six o'clock every morning, and on their separate units, give the prescribed insulin, that Dr. McWilliam would adjust from week to week. The dosage varied from 50 to 1000 units, and they then had to move their patients' bed, and then monitor their coma status. They had help from a psychiatric aide...and it was much later we discovered that he had been injecting these large amounts of insulin right through the

---

17   Doreen Sturla-Scott (2009). *High Hopes – Degrees of Graduation.* Available from Amazon on Kindle.

pajamas! Never any infection! Amazing! Dr. McWilliam would come in at around eight, and be with them the whole morning...Following the coma period, Dr. McWilliam would give at least a hundred cc.'s of glucose intravenously, in a huge fifty cc syringe, which would make them a bit groggy, but able to walk about, bring them out of it, and following a shower, they would eat together, play together, talk about their experiences during the coma, sort of like 'dreaming out loud,' engage in crafts together, go out on walks, and return to their units in late afternoon. (pp. 5-8, Chap. 6)

Sturla-Scott's own assessment of the McWilliam's intervention was that the patients treated "enjoyed a privileged status, and I think a lot of the credit should go to the fact that they received an intensive group therapy, plus the support of one another. I only saw one failure to recover" (p. 6, Chap. 6). When reading such accounts. it can be jarring to think about the seeming ease and "good intentions" that accompanied such acts of physical assault, even if accompanied by the comparative niceties of arranged camaraderie.

Metrazol shock treatment, developed by Hungarian-American neurologist and psychiatrist Landislas Meduna in 1934, replaced insulin with metrazol to induce seizures in schizophrenics in order to increase the presence of glia (the connective tissue of the nervous system), and thereby supposedly reverse the mental disease. About a minute after injection, explosive seizures occurred that sometimes fractured bones and tore muscles. At Ponoka, curare was added to the injections to reduce the violence of the contractions, a procedure that resulted in fewer bone fractures. Injections were given two to three times a week, to a total of between thirty and forty injections. Not surprisingly, after a single episode, patient resistance was considerable, requiring the forcing of further injections until the treatment was completed.

Insulin and metrazol shock treatments were provided at the Ponoka Hospital beginning in 1936, with no recorded indication of the number of patients treated in that year. In 1937, twenty schizo-phrenics were treated with insulin. In his annual report, Dr. MacLean wrote "Results, on the whole, were not considered particularly good, but that was attributed to the fact that unsuitable cases were used. It is expected that better results will be obtained as time goes on and the more hopeful cases are given the treatment." In 1938, both insulin and metrazol were used to treat an unspecified number of patients, and MacLean concluded that "A better type of patient was under treatment than in former years and the results were somewhat more encourag-ing." In 1939, he wrote, "Insulin and metrazol treatments were given, largely under the direction of Dr. Schrag, with encouraging results. It is further shown that best results might be expected in the early cases." It is perhaps telling that these treatments were initiated and continued during the middle to late 1930s, given the low staff to patient ratios and funding shortages at the Hospital. This fact may attest to the desire of Superintendent MacLean to "give fair trial to newer methods of treat-ment and new drug preparations, as accounts have appeared in the literature describing their values." Once again, the juxtaposition of the realities of many of these treatments with what seems to be a genuine concern for patient wellbeing is striking.

It seems clear that the drug-induced shock treatments employed at the Ponoka Hospital in the late 1930s were a far cry from the ideal of a simple and effective physical intervention that would immediately alle-viate patient suffering, decrease treatment time, and reduce demands on busy staff. A modified version of insulin shock therapy continued to be used until the 1950s, sometimes in combination with electroshock therapy, which was introduced in 1943.

• • •

Throughout his time as Medical Superintendent, MacLean continued to advocate and support the work of the Mental Hygiene Clinics, spread across the Province of Alberta, but administered and staffed mostly by the Medical Superintendent of the Ponoka institution. The Mental

Hygiene Movement was begun in 1909 when the National Committee for Mental Hygiene (NCMH) was established in the United States by Clifford Beers, who had experienced life in asylums for the treatment of his bipolar disorder (manic depressive illness) and attempted suicide following the death of his brother. Beers was assisted in his efforts by Harvard psychologist and philosopher William James, and psychiatrist Adolf Meyer. Inspired by Beers' horrific experiences in Connecticut asylums, where he once was placed in a straightjacket for twenty-one days, the NCMH (now called Mental Health America) devoted itself to improving attitudes toward, treatment of, and services for the mentally ill, and promoting mental health in general.

I think one of the most powerfully instructive excerpts from Beer's autobiographical writings[18] is one in which he clearly presents his own perspective when reflecting on one of the many indignities he suffered when being "treated:"

It was not always as an instrument of restraint that the muff was employed [a relic of the Inquisition, the muff was a device used to tether and incapacitate both hands]. Frequently it was used as a means of discipline on account of supposed stubborn disobedience to the attendant...My attendants, like most others in such institutions, were ill-qualified to understand the operations of my mind, and what they could not understand they would seldom tolerate....They thought I was stubborn. In the strict sense of the word there is no such thing as a stubborn insane person...When one possessed of the power of recognizing his own errors continues to hold an unreasonable belief—that is stubbornness. But for a man bereft of reason to adhere to an idea which to him seems absolutely correct and true because he has been deprived of

---

18   Clifford Beers, (1981). *A Mind That Found Itself*. Pittsburgh: University of Pittsburgh Press, p. 19.

the means of detecting his error—that is not stubbornness. It is a symptom of his disease and merits the indulgence of forbearance, if not genuine sympathy. Certainly the afflicted one deserves no punishment. As well punish with a slap on the cheek that is disfigured by the mumps.

As noted in Chapter One, the Mental Hygiene Movement spread to Canada through the efforts of Dr. Clare Hincks. By the 1930s in Alberta, mental hygiene clinics were situated in Edmonton, Calgary, Lethbridge, Medicine Hat, Drumheller, Red Deer, Lamont, High River and the Peace River District, with other areas of the Province occasionally hosting more temporary clinics. Much of the work done in the clinics consisted of investigating cases in the field, and assisting patients and their families—a kind of psychiatric social work initiated by Mr. T. A. P. Frost who was domiciled at the Provincial Mental Hospital at Ponoka. As early as 1929, Mr. Stuart K. Jaffray, also from the Ponoka Hospital, did field investigations and administered psychometric examinations to some patients at the clinics, work that was advanced further by the first psychologist hired at Ponoka, Mr. E. J. (Ted) Kibblewhite, in 1931 at a salary of $200 dollars a month. During the 1930s, more extensive assessments and treatments were offered at the clinics, due to overcrowding in the Province's extended care facilities. Despite this overcrowding and increased workload at the clinics, it was not until after World War II that the Province began to hire more social workers and psychologists at its hospitals and its clinics. During the 1920s and 1930s, only one social worker/psychologist was available at Ponoka. This same individual also rotated through the various clinics, sometimes joined by the Medical Superintendents from Ponoka and the Alberta Hospital Edmonton (formerly the Oliver Mental Hospital).

• • •

Historically, the disciplines and professions of psychology and social work have taken a different view of the nature of mental illness and its treatment from the perspectives predominate in the field of psychiatry. Not being physicians, most psychologists and social workers traditionally have limited themselves to treatments and interventions that are not physically invasive. A few states in America have given psychologists who take extra coursework in pharmacology the legal right to prescribe drugs for treating mental disorders, but this is a recent and limited exception. During the history of modern psychology, dating from the last three decades of the nineteenth century, when psychology became recognized as a separate discipline in universities (distinct from physiology and philosophy), the professional practice of psychology has included a variety of discursive (talking) and social, interactional approaches to the treatment of mental illness. Many of the interventions employed by psychologists have been directed at individuals who are not mentally ill but who are experiencing temporary difficulties related to everyday stress, anxiety, relationships, fears and phobias at home, at work or in their social lives. Social workers are even less likely to employ methods that involve physical intrusiveness than psychologists, and tend to focus on interventions that relate to groups, communities and the social and economic circumstances in which individuals and families find themselves, helping them with their financial and relationship difficulties and assisting them to navigate the institutional arrangements that governments and a wide variety of social agencies have erected to deal with their concerns and struggles.

Having made these general distinctions, it is important to emphasize that the "talking cures" attempted by psychologists also have been used by many psychiatrists. It is not unusual to find psychiatrists, especially in their private practices, as opposed to their work in institutions, who approach their patients and clients with techniques and philosophies of treatment drawn from Freud and other medically-trained psychoanalysts, as well as from non-physician psychologists. The latter include humanistic approaches, such as that of Carl Rogers (person-centred therapies that emphasize "active listening" and emotional support), rational emotive therapeutic methods like those pioneered by Albert

Ellis (which alert clients to the dysfunctional effects of self-defeating and anxiety-arousing thinking and self-talk), and gestalt techniques developed by Fritz Perls (interventions that use role play and encounter with others to encourage self-discovery and emotional release). All of these interventions are non-physically invasive.

Non-physical psychoanalytic methods include free association, memory and dream work, and the tracing and interpreting of sources of clients' and patients' concerns and afflictions in terms of their early life experiences within their nuclear families. Such early sources of difficulty may be revealed through "slips of the tongue" or the nature and location of symptoms (including physical symptoms such as partial paralysis associated with mental illnesses like hysteria). The individual nature, intensity, length and expense of traditional psychoanalytic treatment (the original "talking cure") has meant that it is rarely employed in public institutions for the insane. For those with the means to access and afford such intervention, there always have been private practice and support facilities that offer it at considerable expense to those treated. On the other hand, many of the psychotherapeutic methods developed by psychologists claim to be much less time-intensive and more conducive to shorter-term use with both individuals and groups of patients and clients. It is these forms of psychotherapy that became popular at the Ponoka Hospital during the 1950s, 1960s and into the 1970s.

Most mental health facilities, past and present, have offered and continue to offer biophysical interventions administered, or supervised, by psychiatrists, who as physicians occupy the top rungs in the treatment hierarchies of most institutions for the mentally ill. These interventions are supplemented by the more social, interactive efforts of other staff, including psychologists and social workers, who treat patients with a combination of assistance in navigating everyday life in the institution, planning and following through on plans to modify patients' behaviour in positive directions through a mix of instruction, modeling, reinforcement and encouragement, and occasionally, if time, resources and staffing levels permit, to help a few patients, either individually or in small groups, who seem to be particularly suitable candidates for one or more psychological therapies.

· · ·

Just before and after receiving my Ph.D. from the University of Alberta in 1973, I worked as an institutional attendant at the Ponoka Hospital during the summers of 1968 and 1969, and later as a postdoctoral psychological intern at Cape Breton Hospital in Sydney, Nova Scotia. Like most who begin work in such settings, my initial experiences were ones of trepidation, amazement and bewilderment. Despite my undergraduate and graduate coursework and brief orientations to my duties offered by the institutions in which I was employed, nothing prepared me for actually being on the wards and attempting to perform the various duties that had been assigned to me. Patients sat and walked about in various stages of animation. Some rocked back and forth, talked to themselves or gestured in ways difficult to decipher. Others seemed fixated, perhaps entranced in their inner workings. Every once and a while someone would yell out something, often incomprehensible, or display some other demonstration of upset or excitement.

Nursing staff circulated amongst all of this activity to conduct routine physical checks and usher patients back and forth to various venues for treatment of a wide variety of physical and mental ailments. All of this was the general background within which I and other attendants and ward staff followed a daily schedule of waking patients and assisting them to get washed, bathed and dressed, serving meals to some and accompanying others to dining rooms, readying individuals or groups of patients for stints in one or another centre for occupational or other forms of therapy, and accompanying them to and from these venues. In any way we could, we attempted to be helpful, or at least not to get in the way of more important activities being conducted by nurses and physicians. We assisted individual patients who required help in the bathroom, some of whom had inadvertently or perhaps purposefully soiled themselves. When not otherwise occupied, we attempted to talk to and/or engage one or two patients in some kind of game (mostly cards) or some other activity (e.g., physical movement and exercise), until it was time for lunch, and on and on it went.

Sometimes a bell would ring, signaling a call for assistance elsewhere in the Hospital, and one or more of us attendants would hurry to help with some incident that required additional personnel to restrain a patient and escort him or her to a padded side room where there was less likelihood of harm to the patient or others. If I was working night shift, I tried to help patients who would get up and move around, sometimes into the beds of other patients or to hide and wail in closets, or decide to leave the dormitories for other parts of the ward, or attempt to escape the institution entirely. Every once and a while, a patient died and I, sometimes with another attendant, would be asked to deliver the body to the Hospital morgue, waiting there until one of the on-call physicians or morticians arrived. At other times, we attendants might be asked to accompany patients to electroshock treatment and assist in restraining them while the treatment was administered. I still have the occasional nightmare related to such times, ones that drip with guilt and self-loathing. During reflective, waking moments such as the writing of this paragraph, I experience a bewildering dissociation from these events, as I struggle to square them with my usual sense of myself.

It is not easy to care for a ward of forty to fifty individuals with mental illnesses sufficiently serious to prevent them from being able to function in everyday settings outside the Hospital. Despite my early familiarity with the various patients that my father had brought to our home or to our family gatherings on day passes, being amongst a great number of such people, many of whom functioned far less capably than those with day privileges, was an entirely novel, challenging and sometimes unnerving experience.

• • •

Later, in the mid-1970s at the Cape Breton Hospital on the outskirts of Sydney, Nova Scotia, my duties were strikingly different because of my newly minted status as a Ph.D. psychologist. Instead of spending entire shifts on the wards, I logged much of my time in an office reviewing patient records, conversing with colleagues (psychiatrists, other psychologists, social workers, hospital administrators) and patients and/or members of their families, discussing patients' life histories, progress or lack thereof, and considering treatment plans. I left my office for a daily tour around the wards to meet with "charge nurses" responsible for the running of their particular wards, to observe patients in their "natural habitat," and to make case notes for weekly conferences at which treatment plans for particular patients were reviewed and tweaked. Most of the interventions I planned and supervised were focused on behaviour and cognitive modification in which ward staff were instructed to praise and encourage particular forms of positive social behaviour and ignore or intervene to distract patients from engaging in negative social behaviour. With all this focus on patients' actions and thoughts, together with the constant demands of behavioral or cognitive treatments and therapy, it was surprisingly easy to forget, ignore or somehow overlook the obvious and important fact that they were fellow human beings—possible "me's" occupying other, much less desirable niches within our common human condition. Occasionally, I would be jolted out of my role as a psychologist to contrast my everyday life with situations I encountered when I visited the families and homes of patients. On many of these occasions, it was impossible to ignore or understate the obvious advantages and opportunities I had enjoyed in comparison to those who had grown up and lived in such circumstances.

Like most such institutions during the 1970s, wards in the Cape Breton Hospital psychiatric facility were organized so as to group together patients with similar levels of functioning and with somewhat similar diagnoses, a model of administrative and everyday organization not all that different from that at the Ponoka Hospital. I was never entirely convinced about the wisdom of such a system—imagine, for

example, roomfuls of paranoid individuals as an everyday social environment in a "helping" facility. However, I was unable to think of better
alternatives, given the complexities involved and numbers of individuals to be cared for.

Inevitably, practical considerations related to attempting to ensure
that wards were properly equipped and staffed, that meals and medications could be prepared and delivered in a timely and efficient manner
without errors, and many other such matters typically trumped possibly more therapeutic arrangements like, for example, having less
disturbed patients assist in some aspects of caring for each other, or
allowing patients who showed marked improvement to be accommodated in smaller "cottage wards" to live less institutionalized lives with
a live-in staff member who modeled and supported the self-sufficiency
and effective functioning of members of a small patient "family unit."
Nonetheless, during my time at both Ponoka and Cape Breton, a few
such alternative care models were set up, mostly on an experimental
basis, for selected patients and staff, often including a social worker
or psychologist. Unfortunately, for many patients, especially those
with chronic conditions that attended physical disease, age and dis-
ability, treatment was limited to custodial care that was as beneficent
as possible.

Of course, mistakes were made, in which intended beneficence
quickly morphed into aversive and punitive treatment. One ward at
Cape Breton, as at Ponoka for much of its history, was given over to the
criminally insane, sometimes dangerous individuals who were there
because of court orders following the commission of violent offences.
Such wards typically contained a number of side rooms or actual cells
in which the most violent "prisoner patients" could be housed, separated from others. At Cape Breton in the 1970s, such cells were built
to permit easy observation and monitoring of patient inmates. Having
implemented a behaviour modification program for one such patient,
which was intended to reward him with cigarettes (the "go to" reinforcer
in the 1960s and 1970s) for behaving non-violently whenever he was

removed from his cell to bath or to exercise, I became frustrated by his continued aggression to nurses and attendants who accompanied him on these outings. Eventually, I decided to remove objects like books from his cell/room as a consequence of his physical assaults on staff. Now, anyone who has studied psychology (and/or is possessed of good common sense) will know that such a strategy is a form of punishment, and is likely to enhance, not reduce, aggression and attack behaviour. This remains true even if what is removed is intended to be restored at a later date contingent on non-aggressive conduct, as I had planned to do in this case. When the patient, having once again behaved violently, returned to his cell to find one of his favorite books gone, he literally tore the place apart, injuring himself in the process. Psychological interventions like psychiatric interventions can easily go awry, sometimes with deleterious physical and psychological consequences to patients. And sometimes, such "psychological interventions" may be employed in ways that are more reflective of the psychologist's than the patient's state of mind.

• • •

The foregoing vignette and the manner of its telling betray some of the sense I shared with many of the staff I worked with at Ponoka and Cape Breton that the treatment methods at our disposal paled in comparison with the magnitude of the therapeutic challenge. It also illustrates some of the ways in which patient treatment can be conflated easily with what is good for caregivers. After all, encouraging smoking and treating an adult patient as if he were a child are hardly conducive to the furtherance of personal wellbeing and rehabilitation. The frustration at the therapeutic impotence I experienced in my role as a fledgling institutional psychologist should not have resulted in a desire to punish a patient. In this and other instances, I often found myself infused with a simmering frustration that asked "What the hell am I doing here and what can anyone do here"?

One other story from my days at the Cape Breton Hospital speaks to a broader context for understanding mental illness and its purported treatments. When I, usually accompanied by a social worker who also enjoyed getting away from the Hospital to drive through the picturesque Cape Breton countryside, would visit the homes and families of patients at the Hospital, I was frequently appalled at what I discovered. On one occasion, the place we visited was an unfinished shack, the bottom and only level of which was protected overhead by tarpaper. Inside, the furniture consisted primarily of cases filled with empty beer bottles, piled into some semblance of chairs and beds. Another time, we visited with a mother who tearfully explained to us how she sometimes would place her toddler son in laundry bags equipped with breathing holes and hang him up in the closet when her husband demanded they go out. Suffice it to say that there often are reasons for mental illness that do not require much in the way of psychiatric, psychological or sociological sophistication to fathom. In many ways, I believed then, and I believe now, that what is most impressive about many with mental illness is how resilient, not how disturbed, they are, given the circumstances they have endured.

Another matter related to my "home visits" while at the Cape Breton Hospital concerns the great social and cultural distance that often exists between hospital psychiatrists and other professional caregivers and their patients. Wide gulfs in education and diversity of life experience and perspectives typically exist between professional healers and those they treat, especially in large institutional contexts. These inequalities, mostly the result of differences in social and economic status, often make it extremely difficult for the providers of mental health services to comprehend the actions and lives of those they treat. In the early parts of the twentieth century, there is much evidence that such status differentials were further fueled by widespread and systemic bias, bigotry and stereotyping directed at the poor, the uneducated, the uncultured and the "different." In this context, the accomplishments of Baragar, Davidson and MacLean at the Ponoka Hospital perhaps deserve particular commendation, even if their various attempts to help patients in their care cannot always be aligned easily with contemporary perspectives and assessments concerning appropriate therapeutic concern and care.

. . .

In thinking back to my early experiences in psychiatric hospitals, I am getting ahead of my historical tale. However, I want to remind myself of, and alert readers to, some of the quotidian realities of institutional life and treatment of the mentally disturbed that easily can be passed over without comment when writing about such matters. By the end of the 1930s, the Provincial Mental Hospital at Ponoka had, and continued to, experience the ravages of probably its most harrowing decade. As the 1940s dawned, the Hospital remained overcrowded, underfunded and understaffed. Its physical facilities were deteriorating and qualified staff, always in short supply, were beginning to be lost to the war effort, following the outbreak of hostilities between Fascist Germany and Britain, Canada's Commonwealth leader. The Second World War was to mark a major turning point not only for Canada and the World, but also for the treatment and care of the mentally ill, and the Ponoka Hospital, for better and worse, was at or near the vanguard of such institutional changes.

CHAPTER THREE:
WAR AND ITS AFTERMATH

The Second World War raged from 1939 to 1945. More than a million Canadian men and women served in the armed forces. Forty-three thousand of them never came home. The Canadian war effort began as a limited action in support of Britain and France in their battle against Hitler's Fascist Germany. However, the collapse of France in the summer of 1940 badly frightened Canadians and their leaders, resulting in a vastly expanded commitment to the war that included the federal government's very contentious decision to conscript its citizens into the armed forces. By 1942, there were five Canadian divisions overseas. Full engagement with the enemy occurred in 1943 with the invasion of Sicily by British and Canadian forces.[19]

My father was one of those Canadian infantrymen who followed the taking of Sicily with a continued advance up the Italian boot, which included intensive fighting in and around Ortona. It was in Ortona that he was badly wounded when a tower from which he was sniping was blasted by a German mortar shell. Buried in the rubble, he was

---

19   Information about Canadian involvement in the WWII is supported by various entries in the *Canadian Encyclopedia*, Edmonton, AB: Hurtig Publishers.

recovered and underwent back surgery, after which he remained in action as an assistant medic in the same field hospital unit in which he had been repaired. Eventually he was moved from Italy to France, Belgium and the Netherlands. Just short of 93,000 Canadians served in Italy, and nearly 6,000 lost their lives there. Many more suffered life-long physical and psychological damage.

Haunted by his wartime experiences, my father eventually returned to Canada late in 1946, with a newly acquired fondness for whisky and a propensity for sadness, as the Canadian wartime medical services in Europe gradually disbanded. Upon his return, he, like most of the others who had worked at the Provincial Mental Hospital at Ponoka before heading overseas, was offered employment by the Hospital, in a job that was deemed suitable to his current state of physical and mental health, transferring from the Hospital Farm to its Bakery, where he continued to work until his retirement many years later. The Bakery proved a perfect fit for my father's drinking. Paired with another drinker, who had been appointed head baker, the two men began work at 5:00 each morning, preparing and shoveling great quantities of bread loaves, pastries and pies into the bakery ovens, often assisted by a few patients of the Hospital. In the relative seclusion of their domain, the two bakers felt free to refresh themselves with the occasional pull from a hip flask.

At home, my father's unpredictability increased with the amount he drank—sometimes very little or none; sometimes considerably more, especially if any pals or relatives dropped by. The worst times saw him crying in the basement of our Riverside home clutching a 12-gauge shotgun, the barrel to his chin. At times when his drinking drove him from my parents' bedroom, he slept on one of the twin beds in my room. On more than one occasion, when getting up to relieve myself or arriving home late as a teenager and attempting to sneak into my room, he suddenly, upon hearing some sound I must have made, would roll quickly out of the single bed he used and put me into a combat hold with his forearm across my windpipe and a menacing expression on his face, before just as quickly releasing me to return sobbing to his bed.

In my extended family, such behaviour was not uncommon. Two uncles had served in one of the two Canadian armoured tank divisions during the war, while another uncle also had worked as a field hospital orderly and ambulance driver. All had seen their share of wartime horrors, all drank to excess, and all could behave mercurially on occasion. Once, while sleeping on couches in our grandparents' living room, my cousin and I were jolted awake by a cacophony of fisticuffs amongst my father and uncles that had erupted over a game of poker, fueled by many glasses of whisky. In the morning, one uncle was removed to an emergency ward for stitching and dental work. On another memorable occasion, again at my grandparents, one of my uncles, sleeping on a pullout cot with the hired man—who also had been drinking—thought he detected an intruder in the middle of the night. He grabbed an army issued handgun he had tucked under his pillow, and blew off the big toe of his sleeping partner, a toe which apparently had been responsible for the motion that had conjured the never present intruder—another emergency room trip.

Clearly, by any reasonable standard, my father and several of his friends and relatives were not well. At best, they might be considered functioning alcoholics. Their problems were obviously related to their wartime experiences. Today they would be considered to have been suffering from post-traumatic stress disorder. However, unlike those ex-soldier patients at the Ponoka Hospital at the time, none of them ever graced the wards of that or any other psychiatric facility. They could and did hold jobs, and their families coped as best they could with their drinking and irregularities.

• • •

When considering the 1940s at the Ponoka Hospital, it is helpful to recall the full effect of the war on the civilian population of the country during the early to mid-1940s. Just as things were radically altered for those at the front, everyday life in Canada was also changed in ways that were often quite dramatic, even if generally nonviolent. As the

Canadian war effort ramped up in 1942, the Canadian government established the National Selective Service, which effectively controlled recruitment and assignment of Canadian soldiers, and distribution of labour at home, including where civilians could work, and when they might change jobs. Together with the Wartime Prices and Trade Board, the National Selective Service developed rationing schemes to control the supply and distribution of essentials such as oil and gas, meat and butter, and any other goods in short supply—scarcities produced by the wartime disruption of labour, markets and trade. Inevitably, there was a black market in restricted goods, but the vast majority of Canadians rallied around the war effort and regarded such illicit trade as a social crime.

The irony of wartime with respect to consumer goods was that just when most Canadian families had acquired sufficient purchasing power following the depression of the 1930s, shortages caused by the war meant that there was little to buy. Despite tax increases to support the war effort, many Canadians purchased war bonds in support of the troops. Even school children were urged to buy war stamps featuring tanks or airplanes at twenty-five cents apiece—at the time, a price that would have enabled the contributing child to attend a newly released movie and enjoy popcorn and pop while watching it. Canadian families also collected cooking fat and other useful household waste that could be recycled for military use, planted and harvested "victory gardens" on unused patches of land to secure fresh produce, and collected old pots and pans that could be melted down and used for weaponry.

• • •

At the Provincial Mental Hospital Ponoka, staff and patients also participated in and experienced the consequences of Canada's military and domestic plans. Deteriorating buildings, especially roofs, were given only emergency patching as all members of the hospital community coped with dampness and cold. Portions of the produce and funds generated by the hospital farm and canteen were redirected into care packages for troops, and used to make financial contributions to the armed forces. Several of the hospital physicians and nurses volunteered for wartime service in field hospitals and ambulance services. Despite the end of the Great Depression, the Second World War ensured an inadequate supply of funding, personnel and maintenance to support the Hospital's operation.

From 1940 to 1945, overcrowding and understaffing required constant effort to admit only the most disturbed of an ever increasing, potential number of new patients. The staff shortages meant curtailments in many traditional and more progressive forms of patient treatment (such as occupational therapy and psychotherapy) that made high demands on staff time. The usually detailed paperwork that typically attended patient admissions, the gathering of family histories, the documentation of treatments and their effects, and the recording of many other hospital activities suffered many cutbacks and omissions. So that patients could enjoy reasonably healthy diets during the winter months, a newly expanded Hospital Cannery was kept busy preserving vegetables and fruit grown in expanded hospital gardens that included a new "berry farm." The hospital nursing stations and surgery went into overdrive as the crowded, understaffed wards, now populated by a much higher percentage of aggressively recalcitrant patients, in addition to vulnerable geriatric patients, offered up a steady supply of minor and major ailments, injuries and accidents.

In many ways, the story of the Ponoka Hospital during the war years was one of amazing coping and accomplishment under extremely difficult conditions. The patient population averaged around 1600 until the end of the war, before falling to about 1400 for the remainder of the 1940s. In 1947, the geriatric facility of Rosehaven, located in Camrose, was opened, and it accepted many of Ponoka's vulnerable, elderly patients. Through it all, Superintendent MacLean and his staff worked tirelessly to ensure that despite funding, personnel and resource shortages, things continued to bear some semblance of normalcy. His annual reports to the Department of Health during the war years[20] provide an understated, yet moving testimony to the determination and concern that he and many others demonstrated in managing and directing Alberta's mental health facilities and programs during this time. MacLean's reports also contained sage advice for mental health policy during and beyond the war years, advice delivered not only in his capacity as Superintendent of the Provincial Mental Hospital at Ponoka but, later in the decade, also in his larger role as Acting Director and Chief Medical Superintendent for the Province of Alberta.

• • •

MacLean was an overworked, and highly competent administrator who wore many hats, also overseeing the operations of the mental health facilities at Claresholm and Raymond, as well as being responsible for the Province's Mental Hygiene and Guidance Centres (services that were also disrupted by the war-produced shortages of resources and medical personnel). In addition, MacLean taught courses in psychiatry to the student nurses and attendants in the Training School at Ponoka, as well as to medical interns from the University of Alberta and Graduate interns at both the University and the Ponoka Hospital. In reading his recommendations during the early to mid-1940s, it is easy to imagine the level of frustration he must have experienced when his proposals were consistently ignored by the Province's governing bodies. The one exception was the eventual opening of several new floors for difficult patients at the Alberta Hospital at Oliver, a gradual process that eventually relieved some of the most severe overcrowding at Ponoka.

Among the recommendations made by MacLean that were mostly ignored were suggestions for better deployment of personnel and

---

20   As in the previous two Chapters, much of the information contained in this Chapter comes from the annual reports of the Medical Superintendents. For this chapter, the relevant reports are those submitted to the Provincial Government during the 1940s.

resources. For example, concerning the great numbers of senile patients seeking admission to Ponoka, MacLean opined, "It would seem highly advisable and more economical to place such individuals in buildings of cheaper construction, and staff such institutions with persons who are less highly trained, and consequently not as eligible for high salaries as trained nurses and other personnel." He also argued consistently for the establishment and operation of psychopathic wards in general hospitals at major centres such as Edmonton and Calgary, cities whose residents typically accounted for a third to a half of the yearly admissions to the Ponoka Hospital. Despite the shortages of physicians and nurses due to the war effort, MacLean was adamant that whenever "staff is available," the Province's Mental Hygiene Clinics should "be held regularly and at all scheduled points. Many cases are seen and dealt with in the clinics which might otherwise have to be admitted to institutions for diagnosis and treatment."

Included in MacLean's various portfolios was oversight responsibilities for all of the Hospital's auxiliary and support facilities, which now included the Business Office, the Print Shop, the Cannery, the Carpenter Shop, the Tailor Shop, the Shoe Repairing Department, the Laundry, the Stores Department, the Farm, the Gardens, the Sewing Room, the Kitchen and Dietary Department, the Department of Chief Engineer, the Department of Building Maintenance and the Department of Housekeeping. During the War, the cannery produced up to 23,000 gallons of processed fruit and vegetables a year. The Farm also sold surplus produce to the public and other government operations for a profit of approximately $20,00 a year, a very considerable amount at that time. In 1944, the Farm raised enough turkeys to supply all the hospitals in Alberta. The Print Shop not only served the Hospital, but also supplied printing and binding services to other branches of the Province's Department of Health, and to the King's Printer Department in Edmonton. In all of this, MacLean and his Assistant Superintendent Dr. T. C. Michie proved to be highly effective and frugal, fluidly moving resources and personnel from one Department to another and supplementing Provincial budgets with surplus balances created by several Departments that could market scarce produce and products which were much in demand given wartime shortages.

Despite all the extra work demanded by war circumstances, there is a good deal of evidence from MacLean's reports that hospital morale remained surprisingly good, and a strong sense of community was maintained amongst most staff during the first half of the 1940s. New books continued to be added to the Patient's Library, purchased by proceeds from the Hospital Canteen and its annual Bazaar, which also included contributions from the citizens of Ponoka. Following a long period of absence in which such technology was unavailable to the Hospital, new equipment for projecting "talking movies" was obtained with Hospital-generated funds, and both patients and staff "enjoyed the pictures very much." In addition, great efforts were made to ensure that as many patients as possible could continue to make good use of the amenities of the Hospital grounds—including use of the verandas, and picnics, walks and tennis in the summer; the skating rink, games and occupational studios in the winter.

"Parcels of smokes, eats and other articles were sent to members of the Staff in the Services." Several Hospital physicians and nurses had turned soldier or army medic, and responded with the latest news of their "doings" in both the European and Pacific theatres, regaling those at home with exotic descriptions of Japanese Islands ("barren with a volcano, windy and misty, with a great deal of rain at times"), and the physical exertions of soldiering ("For some of us more used to using other parts of our anatomy, we have discovered muscles in our lower extremities never known to exist.").[21]

• • •

---

21   The excerpts recorded here are from war-time letters written to the Medical Superin-
      tendent at Ponoka by Dr. Tomashewsky and Dr. Brotman, respectively (from the AHP
      archives of the Fort Ostell Museum in Ponoka).

Of course, many patients and employees also suffered from inadequate levels of staffing, funding and the general overcrowding that typified the Ponoka Hospital during the war years—patients who were injured in the congestion, those whose treatments were restricted to simple custodial care, and staff who were overwhelmed by never-ending demands on their time and energy. Although there is no denying the war-inspired camaraderie experienced at certain times, it is most likely that the strain produced by overcrowding, understaffing and under-funding probably outweighed the occasional experience of communal *joie de vivre*.

One also cannot help but reflect on former Superintendent Baragar's admonishment that occupational therapy that extended to patient work in the various auxiliary Departments of the Hospital not be allowed to override the patients' own best interests. It is impossible to imagine that this dictum was applied rigorously to much of the patient work that took place during the war years, especially when the surplus services and produce supplied by Hospital Departments like the Farm, the Cannery, the Print Shop and the Carpentry are considered. In the final analysis, the Hospital and its patients and staff managed to get through the period of the Second World War, but it seems clear that these were difficult years for all concerned. For patients, these were years of restricted treatment and privileges, together with increased demands for their labour. For staff, long hours, low pay and increased responsibility were hardly the stuff of celebration. In a sense, as local historian Earl Roberts described them, the war years at the Hospital could be referred to, in appropriately military fashion, as the years of "Mark Time."[22] And yet, Maclean still managed to introduce an eight-hour workday for hospital staff in 1944, replacing the five twelve-hour days per week that were previously demanded of nursing staff and attendants. No doubt this innovation helped to sustain the morale of many staff members as the War neared its conclusion.

---

22   Earl Roberts' (1973) entry in *Ponoka Panorama* (p. 200).

• • •

In all of this, it is important to remember that the experience of patients in the Hospital was always coloured by the fact that the vast majority of them never wanted to be there in the first place, and for the most part, maintained this attitude throughout their experience of the accommodations and treatments that had been, and continued to be, forced upon them. At one extreme, their ways of coping involved "shutting down" or retreating to their own contemplations, preoccupations and fantasies. At another extreme were those who maintained a kind of wearying defiance, maintaining to anyone who would listen that their presence in the Hospital was the result of a grave misunderstanding or serious injustice, and demanding that they be allowed to leave at once to return to their homes and lives outside the Hospital. Still others resigned themselves to making the best of their unwanted situation, and kept active with crafts[23] such as knitting and embroidery, socializing when they were able to do so, and helping out on the wards by performing routine housework and trying to assist other patients. Some oscillated between retreating, defiance and resignation, depending on their moods, their length of stay and whatever was going on in their ward lives at different times.

There was little information in any of the Hospital records I was able to access to indicate that any patients were truly happy to be where they were. I observed the same kinds of patient responses to their situations some twenty years later during my summer stints as an institutional attendant. The simple fact was that very few, if any, patients wanted to be where they were. Saying this does not negate the many positive interactions and relationships I witnessed between members of staff and patients. It is possible to develop helpful and sustaining ties to others in most life situations. Yet most people are able to exercise a much greater

---

23   The Fort Ostell Museum in Ponoka contains and often displays many wonderful examples of such craft work.

degree of active choice and control over their relationships and lives than patients institutionalized in large mental health facilities.

• • •

When the War ended, expectations were high for improved conditions, a sentiment that resonated with the general mood of optimism and pride of accomplishment that attended the Canadian attitude, in general, following the victory over fascism and fanaticism. Surprisingly, the expected influx of psychiatric cases from returning Ponokans and Albertans who had served in the Canadian Armed Forces in Europe and the Pacific never seemed to materialize at a level that further strained conditions at the Ponoka Hospital, perhaps because so many of their mental injuries were poorly understood by them, their families and mental health professionals at the time.

• • •

There was so much happening during the war years that it is possible to overlook a major innovation in patient treatment that was introduced in 1943. As MacLean describes:

> During the year, an Electro-Shock treatment machine was obtained and replaced Metrazol and Insulin treatments almost entirely. The results obtained from the treatment of patients by this method were very gratifying. Although the best results seemed to be obtained in patients suffering from mood disorders, good results were obtained as well from persons with other conditions, especially those displaying reactions that rendered them difficult of management. In this category, would be the destructive, excited and noisy, homicidal and suicidal, stuporous and the non-eating types.

It is difficult to read this passage without wondering about the extent to which patient management under difficult conditions motivated the apparently widespread use of electroshock therapy immediately following the acquisition of the technical device for its delivery. If so, the introduction and use of this treatment at Ponoka would fit well with long-standing controversies about the effectiveness and ethics of what is still considered by many psychiatrists to be their "go to" treatment, especially in cases of mood disorders such as depression.[24]

• • •

Medical use of electricity has a very long history.[25] In the first century AD, Scribonius Largus, a court physician for the Emperor Claudius, used electric eels to treat the headaches of prominent Romans. Many centuries later, Sigmund Freud considered the use of a form of electro-convulsive treatment after reading about its use by a French physician to treat psychogenetic blindness, and by an English physician to treat depression, but rejected it because he thought it could not produce any long-lasting therapeutic benefits. But none of these earlier forms of electrical shock treatment induced seizures. Typically, only relatively weak forms of electricity were applied to various body parts of patients.

It was only in 1938, following decades of experimentation into the electrical induction of epileptic seizures in dogs without killing them, that two technically proficient Italian psychiatrists, Ugo Cerletti and Lucio Bini, attempted the first electroshock treatment of a human patient who likely suffered from what now would be diagnosed as schizophrenia. The patient, who was treated at a clinic at the University of Rome, was stretched out on a bed and two electrodes were attached to the temples of his shaved head. A rubber pipe enclosed in gauze was inserted into his mouth as a bite blocker. After a first attempt to

---

24   As a further footnote to MacLean's comments, the reader is reminded that occasional use of both metrazol and insulin shock therapies continued at Ponoka well into the 1950s.

25   As mentioned earlier, much of the general historical information contained in this book is drawn from my own lecture notes for my courses in the history of psychology delivered in the Department of Psychology at Simon Fraser University.

administer the treatment failed to produce a seizure, the electrical shock administered was heightened to 110 volts for a fifth of a second. As described by historian of psychology, Norman Endler[26], "the patient entered into the clonic phase of an epileptic attack." His "respiration was arrested, his face became pale and took on a blue tinge, his jaws were clenched in trismus, as in lockjaw, the reflection of the cornea was lacking." After forty seconds, during which "the patient's face was violet and the clonic movements continued…the patient's "pulse decreased to between 35 to 40" beats per minute and "the body muscles then relaxed and the movements started to diminish." At the 48th second, "the patient emitted a deep stertorous sigh, cyanosis diminished, and his pulse became normal." After eleven such treatments, the patient was discharged "in good condition and well oriented."

Endler's interest in the history of electroshock or electroconvulsive therapy was personal, as he too had been treated for depression with electrical shock in 1982, although he received a much more refined, less traumatic from of the intervention.[27] Having met Endler following his recovery, I can attest that he thought the therapy he received was vital to his improved condition, and he claimed to have suffered few, if any, negative effects from his treatment. However, others, like actress Carrie Fisher, would beg to differ. In balancing the benefits and liabilities of her many ECTs, Fisher, while strongly endorsing the effectiveness of the treatments in combatting her stubborn depression, also said "the truly negative thing about ECT is that it is incredibly hungry and the only thing it has a taste for is memory."[28]

At any rate, once out of the bag, electroshock therapy (Cerletti's term) quickly spread beyond Italy. By 1940, it was being used in the

26 Norman S. Endler (1988). "The origins of electroconvulsive therapy (ECT)." *Convulsive Therapy, 4,* 5-23.

27 See Endler's 1982 book-length autobiographical essay *Holiday of Darkness: A Psychologist's Personal Journey Out of His Depression.* New York: Wiley.

28 See Carrie Fisher's 2012 autobiographical book, *Shockaholic.* New York: Simon and Schuster, p. 19.

United States. At the renowned McLean Hospital in a Boston suburb, just three years following the Rome experiment, forty-three patients had received the treatment, with thirty-four of them responding with varying degrees of improvement. Twelve were able to leave the hospital. However, even when patients were strapped to gurneys during the process, their bodies sometimes erupted in extreme contortions, occasionally leading to compression fractures of the spine or dislocated jaws. The early electroshock machines, typically weighing about ten pounds, were clunky, briefcase sized devices with only two calibrations—"low" or "high." Eventually it became clear that electroshock was unable to alleviate chronic schizophrenia, but it did prove useful in combatting depression. Nonetheless, the jolts that were intended to release patients from their "altered states" quickly became known for their brutality, and the way in which they often wiped out patients' memories.

• • •

Today's version of electroshock treatment, electroconvulsive therapy or ECT, is a more civilized approach, but still arguably anything but benign. As described by Professor of Psychiatry Enoch Callaway, "The patient is given an anaesthetic and an airway is established so that oxygen can be given. The EEG is recorded so that the operator can tell when a seizure has been produced. With the patient asleep, his muscles are paralyzed with a curare-like drug, so there is no physical convulsion."[29] Because the induced paralysis prevents spontaneous breathing, the patient is ventilated with oxygen as an electrical current, with controlled waveform and duration, is passed through the head to produce an electrical seizure in the brain, one which is verified by the EEG. When treatment is concluded, the patient stays in a recovery room until fully conscious.

---

29   Enoch Callaway (2007). *Asylum: A Mid-Century Madhouse and Its Lessons about Our Mentally Ill Today* (p. 28). Westport, CT: Praeger.

To this day, no one really knows exactly how electroshock therapy or ECT works to ease depression. For many patients, its alleviating effects are transient, it causes memory difficulties, and, although this is much disputed, perhaps causes brain damage, more generally. Sometimes, the memory loss covers significant periods of a patient's life—in the case of Jonathan Cott, his ECT wiped out fifteen years of memories. Cott writes that "the pact with the devil that is ECT requires that one trade certain memory loss (short-term, long-term or both), possible brain damage, and cognitive dysfunction for the temporary relief of depression."[30] And yet, for some ex-patients like Kitty Dukakis, treated at McLean Hospital (which now performs about 10,000 such operations a year), ECT, in combination with an ongoing treatment with antidepressants to combat side-effects, has made her and her ex-politician husband advocates for this form of treating depression: "Given Kitty's experience…I can't support the notion that you try everything else before you try ECT. Those 17 years before we finally got to ECT were brutal."[31]

. . .

I suspect most of us have had direct experience with depression, either our own, or that of family members and friends. The mother of a close childhood friend of mine was treated for bipolar depression (then called manic-depressive psychosis) in the 1950s and 1960s at the Alberta Hospital Ponoka. Her depression had deepened significantly during a rather messy divorce, (which most divorces were in those days, given the very limited reasons that legally justified such a course of action). An additional requirement was a rather lengthy period of separation before divorce could occur. Custody of her children, and her

30   Jonathan Cott (2005). *On the Sea of Memory: Journey from Forgetting to Remembering* (p. 201). New York: Random House.

31   Katharine Q. Seelye (January 1, 2017). "Beneficiary of electroshock therapy emerges as its leading evangelist." New York Times.

husband's "new family" added extra layers of responsibility and emotional stress to her experiences during this time. Eventually, she suffered a complete break-down and was admitted to the Hospital, almost comatose—both physically and mentally exhausted. After receiving a regimen of rest, antidepressants and electroshock, she recovered sufficiently to be moved to an improvised suite in her parents' home, which was in the same neighbourhood of Ponoka in which I grew up. As a frequent visitor, I was fascinated, appalled and a bit frightened by, and for, her at these times.

Upon leaving the hospital each time, she would sit for hours staring through the windows of her suite, drinking coffee, smoking cigarettes and occasionally reading a book, listening to the radio or a phonograph, or watching television after it became available in the 1950s. Gradually, over a period of several months, she would become more animated, interactive and much like her "old self." Then, after a few more months, she would become very outgoing, occasionally dating and drinking, until her behaviour became increasingly erratic, her moods would shift quickly, and she might eventually be found crying, stretched out on her bed or a couch. All of this, of course, constituted the oscillating phases of her illness as it moved inexorably into another period of deep depression, self-loathing and suicidal ideation. At this point, she would return to the Hospital for another round of electroshock treatments, antidepressants and psychotherapy (when it was available). The somewhat predictable cycle of suffering she endured, with its various signposts, became painfully familiar to her parents and children, who experienced all of this with a foreboding that bordered on its own kind of despair and hopelessness, as cycle after cycle unfolded. I lost contact with my friend and his mother after his grandparents died, and I moved on to the University of Alberta following high school. But I have never forgotten my vicarious sense of frustration and impotence as I observed and interacted with this poor woman and those who loved her. Amongst other things, I developed a strong wish that I would never be similarly afflicted—a wish that now extends to all of those I love, and to others as well.

• • •

Doreen Sturla-Scott[32] provides a personal account of electroshock therapy from her days as a psychiatric nurse at Ponoka in the early 1950s.

> We would conduct patients three times a week, fasted without breakfast, to the dormitory of one of the wards, where two doctors waited, with a big black box by their side, and a rubber mouth-gag in their hand. Staff would escort them to a stretcher, and they would look up at the doctors, close their eyes, and wait. One doctor would put the gag in their mouth, the Head Nurse holding it, and the other doctor turn on the current which carried a one-thirty-third of a volt to the person's brain for a period of $1/16^{th}$ of a second. A nurse on each side would hold down the patient, at the shoulders, the hips, the legs, and the feet, and hold down hard until the grand mal seizure, lasting about forty-five seconds, would wave over the patient. During this time they were not conscious, and after a half-hour or so, would get up and have some breakfast, often grossly confused, and usually having wet themselves. Some were very bloodshot in their eyes, had considerable memory loss, and would have to be told, over and over again, who they were, and where they were…This treatment would go on, three times a week, for twenty, thirty, forty, sixty treatments.

> This form of treatment was also a form of punishment for those persons who were behaviour problems, for one particular doctor who did not like persons who were mentally challenged, would "shock" them, but not enough to lose

---

32   Doreen Sturla-Scott (2009). *High Hopes – Degrees of Graduation* (pp. 9-13). Available on Kindle from Amazon.

consciousness completely, bring them around and "chock" [sic] them again, until they said they would be "good.";...one of the experiments conducted by a psychiatrist that year was on three men given electroshock treatment daily until they were totally infantilized, using a baby bottle, and diapers. Then the men were brought back over several months to a state of normalcy, and became involved in ward programs and psychotherapy. Eventually these three men went home. One man came back in six months, one committed suicide, and the other had a massive heart attack and died about a year later.

To some, electroshock treatment or CVT seems to possess all the trappings of medical expertise and authority. However, the facts that no one really knows how it works or can predict when it will work, and its dangers, limitations and significant side effects, disqualify it as a "magic bullet" akin to antibiotics for particular kinds of physically infectious disease or the X-ray-assisted setting of broken bones. The biophysical bases and mechanisms of many physical diseases are much more clearly and objectively formulated than are the purported, hypothesized physical bases for mental diseases. For all of its physicalist strivings and orientations, psychiatry continues to struggle to establish an objectively verifiable taxonomy that links its diagnostic categories to physical treatments that consistently ameliorate them. As many critics have stated, there likely is no single cause for mental illness, and even particular categories or types of mental distress probably do not have a common cause. Given the strong likelihood of multiple causes and the striking differences between various categories of mental illness, it seems very odd that electroshock or electroconvulsive therapy has been used throughout the history of psychiatry with little concern for either the particular etiology or the exact nature of patients' ailments. This seems especially true for treatments administered during the 1940s to the 1970s in places like Ponoka, when the equipment employed to deliver such treatments was nothing short of "clumsy" by today's standards, and patient management and staff convenience sometimes seemed to trump therapeutic treatment as a Hospital priority. As noted by Sturla-Scott, staff and physician convenience also were reflected in the not infrequent threat to use electroshock as a form of patient discipline for disruptive, inappropriate or simply annoying behaviour.

• • •

Yet another set of physical treatments introduced at the Ponoka Hospital immediately post-War were surgeries to the brain that also were intended to interrupt and eliminate patients' maladaptive, dysfunctional thoughts, or at least render patients physically and socially quiescent. Prefrontal lobotomies or leucotomies are attempts to reduce the emotional and cognitive chaos of mental disorder that harken back to ancient practices of trepanation. In the 1930s, undeterred by the almost complete failure of the ancient method, Portuguese physician and neurologist Antonio Egas Moniz argued that mental illness was entirely a neural condition that potentially might be alleviated by damaging parts of the brain that seemed to be implicated in mental dysfunction. Believing that calming patients' turbulent emotions held the key to their cure, Moniz was excited after attending a lecture in London during which a Yale neurologist commented that often when the brain's frontal lobes were damaged those afflicted became subdued emotionally, but displayed little or no cognitive disruption.

Returning to Lisbon, Moniz began to experiment with creating lesions within the frontal lobes of individuals with severe mental disturbance. Placing patients under general anesthesia, Moniz had neurosurgeon Pedro Almeida Lima operate on twenty such patients by drilling two holes, one above each eye and then inserting a syringe-shaped instrument Moniz had invented (a "leucotome") to carve out a small core of brain tissue. Cores continued to be removed until the patient ceased being disruptive. Moniz claimed seven successes, six improvements, and seven failures (in which patients remained unchanged)— results that were disputed by Portugal's leading psychiatrist, José de

Matos Sobral Cid, who observed all of Moniz's patients and described them as actually exhibiting cognitive and personality degradation and quietude attributable to shock and damage. Unapologetic, and consistent with his strongly-held biophysical determinism, Moniz theorized that his leucotomies cured patients by eliminating their functional fixations (i.e., tendencies to perform the same activity over and over). Cid lambasted Moniz's theory as sheer cerebral mythology. Nonetheless, Moniz's treatment was widely heralded as a miracle cure and became popular with asylum psychiatrists struggling with the management of disruptive, hostile patients. "After a relatively simple surgery, endlessly troublesome patients could be rendered docile and obedient."[33]

American neurologist Walter Freeman, also believing that mental illness was caused by overactive emotions, and thinking that Moniz's approach could be adapted and simplified for the benefit of many more mentally disturbed individuals, championed a much simpler surgery— the transorbital lobotomy that could be performed in doctors' offices without the need for a specialized surgeon or a well-equipped operating room. The physician simply lifted the patient's eyelid and slid a surgical instrument resembling an ice pick under the raised lid until meeting a tiny bone at the back of the eye-socket. A small mallet then was used to hammer the pick through the bone and cranial cavity into the brain, rotating the pick to create a frontal lobe lesion. It is estimated that Freeman performed two and a half thousand such procedures before his death in 1972.

For his part, Egas Moniz received the Nobel Prize for Medicine in 1949. Like malarial cures, leucotomies and lobotomies were popular with Nobel committees, even if both perhaps merely reflected the desperation of psychiatrists for a biologically-based quick fix that might relieve families, caregivers and institutional staff of the problems of managing highly volatile and difficult individuals, and to increase their

---

33   In Jeffrey A. Lieberman (2015). *Shrinks: The Untold Story of Psychiatry* (p. 163). New York: Little Brown and Company.

gratitude to and esteem for the purveyors of such fixes, thus enhancing the status and prestige of psychiatry itself. In fairness, there can likely be no doubt about the sincere desire of some who practiced such interventions to help their patients. Nonetheless, any such beneficent desires must be set against the obvious physical intrusiveness of such treatments when received by individuals who most often were not in any position to resist those who delivered them.

• • •

At the Provincial Hospital of Alberta at Ponoka, the post-war years (1946-1949) inspired renewed optimism about the future for the Hospital, its patients and its staff. The Depression and War years were finally over. In his annual report for 1946, MacLean was able to celebrate the appointments of two new medical officers, even while bemoaning the fact that "the countrywide shortage of female nurses and female help generally was felt by the Hospital." In 1947, there was a further "improvement in medical staff numbers" such that "more clinical work was possible and there was a decided increase in the number of *special treatments* given (italics added)." In 1948, the teaching staff at the Nurse's and Attendant's Training School was "brought up to full strength by the addition of two qualified instructors." However, there "still was a shortage of graduate nurses" despite "some improvement in the general staff situation."

The nature of the "special treatments" referred to by MacLean included dramatic increases in the numbers of patients receiving electroshock treatments, sometimes combined with insulin shock treatment, and a further growth in individual patient treatments of all kinds, now that staffing had been restored to more functional levels. All of this was accompanied by a steady decline in the numbers of neurosyphilitic patients treated by both malarial fever and typhoid vaccine fever treatments, now combined with or replaced entirely by penicillin injections. Use of hydrotherapy, physiotherapy and occupational therapy was expanded to include more patients. A wider range and combination of these therapies were administered by better trained and supervised staff. A limited, unspecified number of prefrontal leucotomies was performed. Also in evidence was a steady increase in the numbers of elderly patients experiencing dementia and senility, with an attendant increase in fractures and mostly minor physical injuries to this growing segment of the patient population. These trends and patterns continued throughout the post-war 1940s.

There was also a noteworthy "expansion of mental health services provided by the Provincial Guidance Clinics" (the previous Mental Hygiene Clinics) during this period, much of which also was under the supervision of Dr. MacLean and his Assistant Superintendent at Ponoka, Thomas Michie. With the expansion of a full time Guidance Clinic in Edmonton and additions to the Calgary Clinic, it was possible to provide services to a much larger part of the Province. There was also "an increase in General Public Education activities through radio talk shows, round-table discussions with interested groups, and talks to various school organizations." In 1947, Clare Hincks, Chairman of the National Committee on Mental Hygiene, in another of his exhaustive studies of the Province of Alberta's mental institutions, concluded overall that they had "attained a creditable standard of humanitarian care." In 1949, the Province of Alberta finally acted on another recommendation repeated in Hincks' various reports, and construction was begun on a new psychiatric ward at the University of Alberta Hospital in Edmonton, with occupancy slated for 1951. No work was yet begun on a similar facility at the Calgary General Hospital "for which plans were drawn up some years ago."

On the non-medical side of the Hospital's operations, natural gas arrived at the powerhouse in 1948, the same year a new dormitory to house eighty working patients was completed on the Hospital farm. A new Hospital laundry was added in 1949. Also in 1948, Dr. MacLean formally handed the reins of the Superintendency of the Ponoka Hospital to his assistant, Dr. Thomas Michie. Despite retaining an office at Ponoka as Director of the Alberta Division of Mental Health until his retirement to the Ponoka community in 1965, it seems clear that MacLean did not interfere with the ways in which Michie chose to operate what was now his Hospital.

• • •

Dr. Thomas C. Michie was educated at the University of Alberta, after which he was awarded a fellowship to study at the Mayo Clinic in Rochester, Minnesota. Michie shared, with Baragar and MacLean, a desire to make his mark as a progressive psychiatrist, but primarily through scientific innovation in the treatment of the mentally ill. Under Michie's superintendency, use of physical restraint and seclusion, which had been mostly banned under MacLean, began to creep back into staff practices at the Ponoka Hospital. Michie believed such methods made it easier and safer for staff who were required to care for patients, some of whom could be difficult to manage. These methods also made available more time for staff to assist with innovative therapeutic practices such as electroshock therapy and leucotomies. Michie's primary ambition was to assist psychiatry to achieve a more respected scientific status. He shared Moniz's and Freeman's view that if a patient's mind could be rendered a clean slate, unhealthy thinking could be eradicated so that the patient might acquire new skills for coping in more typically functional ways.

In some ways, Dr. Michie's belief in the possibility of new and startling psychiatric advances in the treatment of the mentally ill was in perfect keeping with a post-WWII belief in and commitment to technological innovation for better living in general. If there was one thing the war had achieved, it was to bring home a convincing demonstration that victory and progress could be achieved by harnessing the best technological means available. Having observed first-hand the horrific consequences of the war for those who died and were injured and maimed—some of whom now returned to Ponoka and its famous Hospital—many were anxious to put the war years behind them. Post-war enthusiasm abounded for technologically advancing "the good life" for both societies and the individuals who populate them. In Canada and the United States, most politicians and members of the general public were anxious to use and enjoy new inventions and ways of "getting things done" that had grown out of the war effort.

• • •

One of the biggest winners when it came to reaping positives from the war was psychology. In many ways, both it and Canada had enhanced their status through war-time contributions. Now it was time to put such contributions and the pride and respect associated with them to work to build a better world—a world full of post-war babies, an economy buoyed by a better equipped and more skilled workforce, and a widespread belief that anything could be accomplished with sufficient effort and "know how." Just how the mentally ill might fare in this new climate of optimism and confidence remained to be seen, but some foresaw great change and renewal here as well.

During the war, psychiatrists and psychologists had used their ideas, tests and interventions to help select, place, train and treat military personnel, advise governments, boost civilian morale and install a general "can do" attitude in many of its growing number of adherents and followers. Post war psychology and a psychiatry based on human functioning, rather than or as much as on disease, were ready to take on traditional psychiatry and push for a greater portion of the financial rewards and status afforded to improved mental health care. Canada, too, had a new respect, not just within the British Commonwealth, but within the family of nations writ large. Canada and its people had punched well above their weight during the conflict, and Canadians and many others looked to the new Canada to step increasingly into the limelight, as a distinctively international presence at industrial, financial, scientific, social service and educational tables worldwide. Canada and its institutions, including the Ponoka Hospital, were ready for renewal, change and renown. As Alan Gregg put it in a 1944 article to psychiatrists and psychologists, in which he anticipated a growing need for psychiatry and psychology when the war ended:

> There will be applications far beyond your offices and hospitals of the knowledge you will gain, applications not only to patients with functional and organic disease, but to the human relations of normal people—in politics, national and international, between races, between capital and labour, in government, in family life, in education, in every form of human relationship, whether between individuals or between groups. You will be concerned with optimum performance of human beings as civilized creatures.[34]

---

34   Alan Gregg (1944). "A critique of psychiatry." *American Journal of Psychiatry, 101*, p. 291.

CHAPTER FOUR:
RENEWAL AND CHANGE

Compared to the almost complete absence of facilities and services available to those returning home from the First World War, Canada did a much better job providing social, educational and apprenticeship programs to its World War II veterans to help them readjust to civilian life. Post-war, many couples married at young ages and raised four or more children. Women were encouraged to be homemakers and mothers. Many who had worked outside the home during the war now stayed in their houses and performed domestic duties, often making way for returning veterans to re-enter the work force. Food and finances that had been depleted by the war effort were suddenly and readily available to support a burgeoning population. Ontarians experienced a manufacturing boom; Albertans reaped the benefits of oil and gas. New homes and automobiles were on display and life for many Canadians had seldom looked so good.

• • •

My wife and I had the good fortune to be born in 1950—members of the post-war "baby boom" generation—into a time and place in which optimism and possibility were in the air. Nonetheless, the war left its marks on many veterans and their families. Life in public sometimes differed dramatically from the private lives of families like my own. Oscillations in my father's mood and demeanour were obvious to me even as a young child. When you are not sure how someone you love will react to you, you learn quickly to notice any signs that might signal how best to approach him, or not. And, of course, with increasing age and experience, you begin to wonder why people behave as they do. You want to understand, not just co-exist. It did not take me long to recognize, even to predict, his drinking patterns. But especially when "in his cups," my father could be far from predictable. And it was obvious that there were other things that perhaps the drinking was intended to keep at bay—deep sadness, regret and guilt. It is not unusual for ex-soldiers to feel guilty and ashamed. After all, they survived when many they thought were better people did not.

Life with my father made me a careful observer, not only of my father but of my mother, other relatives, neighbours and friends. It has been said by many psychologists that the more you understand others and how they react to you, the more you understand yourself. I certainly recall thinking a great deal about my family and myself. I often wished my family was happier, although I also recognized that, overall, we were not exactly unhappy. We just had our difficult times. Would my father have benefitted from any of the forms of treatment offered at the Ponoka Hospital during the 1950s? I have no idea. Perhaps some of the group psychotherapy that was offered to patients and their families might have been of some help. But I doubt very much that my father would have benefitted from any of the physically invasive treatments commonly dished out to patients at the Hospital, including the new drug therapies that were to have so much impact on the future of the Hospital itself. Nonetheless, there certainly were times when I wished I had a pill I could give my father so he would just fall asleep until he woke up sober.

• • •

As it was for post-war Canada generally, the first half of the 1950s was a time of renewal for patients, staff and facilities at the Provincial Mental Hospital Ponoka. The Annual Reports of Hospital Medical Superintendents for 1950 to 1955[35] reveal a number of trends in patient admissions, patient treatments, levels of staffing, and expansion and maintenance of facilities that reflected the general spirit of the times as it settled on the Hospital. During this period, patients in residence at the Hospital numbered approximately 1,500 to 1,600. However, an expansion of medical and treatment staff ensured that patient care and treatment were maintained at a level commensurate "with accepted standards."

Each year from 1950 to 1955, new patients admitted to the hospital ranged between approximately 80-160 voluntary admissions, 130-170 admissions by medical certificate, 330-400 by warrant of the Provincial Attorney General, and at most, ten under *The Mental Defectives Act*. Total annual admissions varied from around 600 in 1951 and 1952, to approximately 700 in 1952, 1953 and 1954, increasing to 730 in 1955. Each year, approximately 500 to 550 patients were discharged, while others were transferred from Ponoka to other Provincial facilities and still others died from a variety of causes at a rate not untypical of death rates in the general public at the time. After 1951, all patients with tuberculosis were transferred to the Provincial Mental Institute, Edmonton (previously Oliver).

Overcrowding was still a problem, but the addition of new patient accommodations helped to reduce its worst effects. Eastview, a cottage style building, was constructed in November, 1952 as an unlocked ward housing male working patients. A similar facility, Dawnview,

---

35   Reports for 1950 and 1952 were written and submitted to the Provincial Government of Alberta by Randall R. MacLean, Director of Mental Health for the Province of Alberta. Reports for 1953 to 1955 were written and submitted by Thomas C. Michie, Medical Superintendent for the Ponoka Hospital. All material quoted is drawn from these reports unless otherwise noted.

opened in 1954. In 1955, an older accommodation for male patients was renovated and refurbished for female patients. Each of these new, open wards housed ninety to one hundred patients. In addition, more and more patients were given ground privileges, until by 1955, twenty-five percent of the total patient population could come and go more or less as they pleased from their wards to their work places, or to enjoy the well-cultivated and expansive hospital gardens and paths. Inside the wards, a small number of television sets became available for patient use in 1955.

The numbers of patients discharged reflected the increasing status of Ponoka as an active treatment facility. In their annual reports, Dr. MacLean, in his capacity of Director of Mental Health Services for the Province of Alberta, or Dr. Michie, as Medical Superintendent of the Ponoka Hospital, consistently remarked that the clinical treatment program "was active and every effort was exerted to keep abreast of new developments," which included "widespread use of Electric and Insulin Shock Therapies." When in 1955, a patient death was caused by "a circulatory failure" during electroshock therapy, Dr. Michie noted that "this was the first death recorded at this hospital in approximately 6,000 patients treated by electroshock." An increasingly small number of neurosyphilitics was admitted at the beginning of the decade, until in 1952, "Malarial Fever Therapy was abandoned and the administration of antibiotics substituted." New lab facilities and staff helped to ensure that "The patients were given the advantage of all necessary diagnostic and treatment facilities." Each year a number of prefrontal lobotomies were performed, with "some encouraging results."

Occupational and Recreational Therapy were extended significantly, especially for newly admitted patients, so as to encourage more rapid rehabilitation and normalization of their conditions. Many of the new occupational therapy offerings were social and psychological treatments in the form of crafts, including new programs centred around organized painting classes. Many patients continued to work in hospital support facilities, but even here, greater concern was given to the therapeutic appropriateness of such placements. For example, female patients who worked in the hospital's Beauty Parlour took pride in assisting parlour operators to provide "nearly 8,000 procedures" each year to as many patients as possible. Such occupational placements were viewed as "stimulating recovery" more generally because of the structured social interactivity they afforded to participating patients. Expanded patient treatments in the form of Recreational Therapy, together with Physical Training, became an increasingly "important factor in promoting contentment, and a feeling of well-being in the patient population."

In addition to hiring more staff to deliver occupational and recreational therapy, a new psychologist and social worker were hired. The latter was the first fully trained social worker to be employed at the Hospital. Whereas previous hospital psychologists (of which there was only one at any given time prior to the 1960s) were limited to providing psychometric assessment at the hospital and the Provincial Guidance Clinics, the new psychologist also conducted individual and group psychotherapy, taught in the School of Nursing and participated as a member of multi-disciplinary treatment teams. Nonetheless, the vast majority of active psychotherapy was offered by psychiatric nurses and attendants, many of them trained by the psychologist and others at the School of Nursing, which continued to turn out five to ten qualified psychiatric nurses and psychiatric attendants each year, in addition to providing four to eight-week courses and programs in psychiatric nursing to student nurses from a variety of Alberta hospitals. The social worker conducted home visits and assessments for persons remanded for psychiatric observation and for outpatients who were being treated at the Hospital but remained in their homes outside the Hospital. The Provincial Guidance Clinics provided follow-up services, including the delivery of medications, to outpatients and ex-patients in the area surrounding the Hospital, and advocated for humane and fair treatment of patients and their families and estates. In his annual report for 1954, Dr.

Michie was able to describe the new treatment policy of the Hospital in the following terms:

> The policy has been toward a gradual and general improvement in the Hospital services. The effort has been directed toward exposing the patients, as far as possible, to normal life contacts, and to so encourage and promote their return to society.

• • •

New therapies to arrive on the treatment scene by 1955 were psychotherapy, especially group psychotherapy, and the use of tranquilizing drugs. Although the former clearly fitted Michie's stated intention for forms of patient treatment aimed at social contact, normalization and reintegration, the latter was to prove much more consequential. Group psychotherapy was a non-invasive treatment supplied mostly by trained psychiatric nurses. It stood in stark contrast to the biologically invasive interventions, such as lobotomies and insulin shock therapy, still being administered at the hospital, also with the enthusiastic support of Dr. Michie.

Psychotherapy as a cure for mental illness is most often traced to the medical practice of Sigmund Freud, located in his residence at Berggasse 19 in Vienna. In late nineteenth century Vienna, mental illness was a label applied to hysteria (a multi-faceted disorder in which psychological stress is converted into physical symptoms that include displays of selective amnesia, volatile emotionality and dramatic forms of attention seeking), neurasthenia (emotional disturbance characterized by fatigue, head and face pain, irritability, and lassitude), sexual perversion and violent criminal behaviour such as rape and murder. Freud and some of his contemporaries understood the causes of such ailments to reside in uncontrollable and uncivilized impulses located in the unconscious minds of those suffering them. After experimentation with hypnosis, cocaine and a variety of other forms of intervention,

Freud famously settled on a "talking cure," through which patients were gradually helped to understand the onset of their symptoms as related to traumatic events, typically experienced in childhood, but repressed from their conscious awareness. Using methods of therapeutic listening, free association, emotional re-experiencing, gradual reconstruction of repressed events and education in psychoanalytic principles and understandings, Freud claimed considerable success in curing and rehabilitating many of his patients.

Other therapeutic approaches to mental illness offered in the late nineteenth and early twentieth century included a wide variety of religious and spiritual practices such as mesmerism, mind-cure philosophy, positive thinking, Christian Science and the Emmanuel Movement (an early form of moral treatment advanced by the Emmanuel Church in Boston). Central to all these early forms of "psychotherapy" was "the doctrine…that individuals suffered from inner emotional or spiritual ills that were caused by personal inadequacies and spiritual deprivation, not by the political and economic conditions of their lives."[36] Whereas many prominent European physicians such as Cesare Lombroso saw mental illness as an eruption of degenerative traits or instincts, some Americans like George Beard, a close friend of Thomas Edison, theorized that mental illness was caused by environmental stress that depleted the brains of sensitive souls of sufficient energy to navigate the demands of everyday and vocational life. Beard's proposed cure was rest, mild electrical stimulation and calmly delivered moral exhortation. Where Freud championed psychoanalytic rechanneling of mental energies from the unconscious mind to the active control of the conscious mind, Beard sought to replenish and free his patients' depleted cerebral energies to enable a return to normal functioning.

---

36   Philip Cushman (1992). "Psychotherapy to 1992: A historically situated interpretation." In Donald K. Freedheim (Ed.), *History of Psychotherapy: A Century of Change* (p. 32). Washington, DC: American Psychological Association.

Throughout the twentieth century, the further development of psychotherapy coincided with attempts to extend the knowledge claims and practices of various schools of psychology to the therapeutic treatment of individuals and groups of individuals experiencing psychological concern, discomfort and disturbance. Prime examples included behaviour therapy and behaviour modification, supported by the work of early behaviourists like John B. Watson, and extended greatly by the work of later behaviourists like B. F. Skinner; the person-centred, experiential and existential therapies advocated by humanistic psychologists like Carl Rogers, Abraham Maslow and Rollo May; more social, interpersonal forms of psychodynamic therapy advanced by Alfred Adler, Harry Stack Sullivan, Melanie Klein and D. W. Winnicott; and the cognitive and cognitive-behavioural therapies pioneered by Donald Meichenbaum, Albert Ellis and Aaron Beck.[37]

• • •

At Ponoka, the form of group therapy most commonly practiced during the 1950s was an eclectic mix of a somewhat directive form of Carl Rogers' "active listening" therapy to facilitate patients' communication of their concerns to the group leader and other patients, augmented by interpersonal role play and social behavioural skill training, all spiked with whatever personal therapeutic strategies and styles were favored by individual group leaders, sometimes including plans for behavioural change and maintenance that involved other hospital staff and extended to interactions on the wards. The occasional staff member or group leader also might have employed psychoanalytic or psychodynamic interpretation and suggestion, depending on her or his personal knowledge and ability. Many of the psychiatric nurses

---

37   Most of the information provided here concerning the history of psychiatry, psychology and psychotherapy is drawn from my lecture notes and supporting materials collected and developed during my years of teaching the history of psychology at Simon Fraser University.

and attendants who offered such social psychological interventions were taught these and other methods of group facilitation during their training at the Hospital's Nursing School. Here, more dramatic forms of group therapy involving emotionally expressive, interpersonal encounter and gestalt psychotherapy (as practiced by Fritz Perls) were also taught. Later, especially in the 1960s, as part of their training, group leaders themselves participated in longer, more intensive forms of group therapeutic retreats, sometimes at the Hospital, but often at various therapeutic centres and communities located elsewhere in Alberta and beyond.

• • •

Despite the success many at the Hospital attributed to group psychotherapy, by the mid-1950s, psychopharmaceutical drugs began to dominate the psychiatrist-controlled treatment of most of the patients at the Ponoka Hospital and similar institutions. This new form of invasive therapy would eventually replace insulin shock therapy and reduce greatly the frequency of electroshock and psychosurgery. Like fever, coma and shock treatments, early uses of drugs in psychiatry were "blunt instruments for pacification."[38] Morphine and other opiate-derived drugs had been used in late nineteenth century asylums to manage difficult and aggressive patients. Around the same time, the first behaviour altering or psychotropic drug, chloral, a sleep-inducing non-opiate, was introduced to relieve insomnia. Both early opiate and non-opiate drugs were not targeted at the relief of particular patient symptoms or the causes of these symptoms. They were used as knock-out drugs that proved to have the significant side-effect of inducing addiction. Chloral likely was the drug involved in the origination of the expression, "slipping someone a mickey," after famed Chicago bartender Mickey Finn, who added what is believed to have been chloral

---

38   Jeffrey A. Lieberman (2015). *Shrinks: The Untold Story of Psychiatry* (p. 173). New York: Back Bay Books.

to the drinks of customers he intended to rob. English writer Virginia Woolf used chloral to treat her manic-depressive illness. Woolf wrote to her lover Vita Sackville-West about her reactions to the drug:

> Goodnight now, I am so sleepy with chloral simmering in my spine that I can't write, nor yet stop writing—I feel like a moth, with heavy scarlet eyes and a soft cape of down—a moth about to settle in a sweet bush—would it were—ah, but that's improper.[39]

Of course, knocking patients out reduced their symptoms. It is difficult to act in any way—paranoid, anxious, manic or aggressive—when asleep. Nonetheless, psychiatrists reasoned that perhaps the administration of the right types of drug might induce a kind of sleepy wakefulness that would usher disturbed patients into a calm, relaxed and biddable state. Enter drugs like sodium bromide, which Scottish psychiatrist Neil Macleod claimed could, after inducing prolonged sleep, remove patients' troublesome symptoms for days or weeks. Getting the dose right was critical to the avoidance of cardiovascular events and respiratory distress and even then, toxin build-up in the liver increased with each dose taken. Despite such liabilities, sodium bromide swept through many asylums, being cheaper to produce and more powerfully effective than choral. As evidence of its risks finally became too great to be tolerated, the use of sodium bromide was discontinued.

The first drug that was developed and demonstrated to redress particular symptoms so that a patient might be discharged into normal life—i.e., the first psychopharmaceutical drug—was meprobamate, the effects of which were deemed tranquilizing, in that the drug reduced anxiety without inducing sleep. Needless to say, meprobamate, initially marketed as Miltown, sold like hotcakes, with thirty-six million prescriptions filled by 1956. Although celebrated in the Rolling Stone's 1966 song "Mother's Little Helper," by that time, most psychiatric use

---

39   Lieberman (2015), p. 174.

of meprobamate had given way to a new generation of psychophar-maceuticals, including Librium and Valium, which today have in turn been eclipsed by benzodiazepines like Xanax. Despite removing many symptoms of anxiety, meprobamate itself did little to relieve patient's experience of hallucinations, painful sadness or disorganization as they sat, now more calmly, in asylum wards at Ponoka and other institutions.

The drug that really kick-started the psychopharmaceutical revolu-tion in asylum psychiatry was the antihistamine chlorpromazine, used initially by French surgeon Henri Laborit to reduce the shock of antici-pated surgery. Anxious patients who received the drug became indiffer-ent to imminent operations. Eventually, Laborit was able to convince psychiatric colleagues to try his drug on psychotic patients. When administered intravenously to a violently hallucinating twenty-four-year-old individual on January of 1952, the patient, following three weeks of continuous treatment, was calm and able to return to normal social and vocational activities. His hallucinations, delusions and dis-organized thoughts were simply gone. Subsequently, several others, also treated with the drug, described how their hallucinations gradu-ally became more and more distant and receded into a non-distressing background. Needless to say, chlorpromazine was hailed as a miracle drug that immediately became adopted throughout Europe. Marketed in North America as Thorazine and promoted as a way of cutting costs of asylum care by enabling more patients to be treated quickly and effectively, and returned to society, it revolutionized not only patient treatment, but raised the possibility of much shorter periods of hospi-talization for many suffering mental illness.

When, in 1958, Geigy pharmaceuticals released imipramine, one of a new class of drugs called tricyclic antidepressants, that seemed to treat depression with a level of success equal to or even greater than that achieved through Thorazine treatment of psychosis, the profession of psychiatry was once again revolutionized. Only manic-depressive illness now seemed untreatable and unmanageable. But when little known Australian physician John Cade used lithium carbonate to great success as a way to replenish deficiencies of lithium in manic patients, psychiatry possessed seemingly effective psychopharmaceutical treatments for what many psychiatrists considered the three main strands of mental illness: antipsychotics (like Thorazine) for psychosis, antidepressants (like imipramine) for depression, and mood stabilizers (like lithium) for mania.

• • •

The impact of these new drugs is difficult to imagine for anyone unfamiliar with daily life on the wards of psychiatric hospitals before 1955.[40] For many staff at the Ponoka Hospital, there was a new sense of optimism that related directly to their arrival and use.

> The newest, and most promising development in the active treatment of mental illness is that of chemotherapy, or the use of drugs...The "pictures" painted of them...in popular magazines like MacLean's and The Readers Digest [are] perhaps too rosy. Nevertheless, it is a tremendous stride forward! The century-old dream of physicians and public alike is coming true. At long last there is a basis for genuine hope—for a cure for the worst affliction of man—the cruel contrary cross of mental illness. Perhaps the day is dawning when, with improved drugs and other technique[s], the mental institutions, as we have known them will be no more.[41]

Suddenly, Hospital staff could devote more of their time and energies to active patient treatment, freed from much of the labour-intensive,

---

40   Readers interested in a much more nuanced and complete discussion of these matters might want to consult John Gach's (2008). "Biological psychiatry in the nineteenth and twentieth centuries," in Edwin R. Wallace IV & John Gach (Eds.), History of Psychiatry and Medical Psychology (pp. 381-418). New York: Springer.

41   From an unpublished memoir entitled, A Brief Outline of the Ponoka Mental Hospital, authored by D. J. Crowley, an attendant employed at the Ponoka Hospital from 1932 to 1954. This document is housed in the archives of the Fort Ostell Museum in Ponoka, Alberta.

continuous tasks of basic caregiving, which now could be given back to previously incapacitated patients who seemed to have recovered sufficiently to care for themselves.

With the new drugs, institutionalized patient populations went into decline, and psychiatrists and governments began to rethink how psychiatric patients should be treated. Old standards like shock therapies, with the exception of ECT for severely depressed and suicidal patients, mostly went the way of the dodo by the late 1960s. Nonetheless, somewhat muting the understandable euphoria that attended the psychopharmaceutical breakthroughs of the 1950s, were rumblings of troubling side-effects experienced by many patients—side-effects that often seemed to prevent deinstitutionalized former patients from adhering to their prescribed drug regimens. Moreover, there was a worrisome lack of understanding of the exact biological mechanisms by which many of the new drugs achieved their results—a concern that continues to this day, and has led many critics to be suspicious of what else might be happening to, and/or troubling, patients treated with them. As we shall see in the next chapter, it was this concern, in addition to the continuing involuntary incarceration and forced treatment of psychiatric patients in many jurisdictions, that fueled the anti-psychiatry movement of the 1960s.

• • •

An example of the experiential effects that can accompany the taking of psychopharmaceuticals is provided by Ann Bolo, a thirty-five-year-old painter and social worker struggling with postpartum depression, who was prescribed Prozac.[42]

---

42   The case of Ann Bolo is reported by Lauren Slater in her 2018 book, *Blue Dreams: The Science and the Story of the Drugs that Changed our Minds.* New York: Little, Brown and Company, pp. 169-179. Prozac was not developed until 1972, but the "dulling effect" reported by Bolo is a common side-effect of many psychopharmaceuticals used to treat anxiety, depression, and other mental disorders.

On Prozac, far fewer things bother me. I'm like a Teflon-coated pan. What would have stuck to me before now just falls off me. I'm more superficial than I was before. I saw a movie the other day with a friend. Off Prozac, I would have cried at the end. On Prozac, I'm dry-eyed. Everyone else in the movie theater was weeping except me. I call it the "so what" side effect. It worries me a little bit, but on the other hand, I'm so relieved not to be depressed that I'm willing to live with what I call my "Martha Stewart self."

Bolo also reported sexual side effects: "If I were a guy, I'd describe it as having intercourse with a sock on. I don't think I'm a hundred percent numb, but I'll bet I'm seventy-five percent numb…My sexual desire has diminished to almost zero." For some, the "dulling effect" they report experiencing with their ingestion of psychoactive drugs is a fair trade for the reduction of their debilitating anxiety or depression. However, Lauren Slater, who reported Bolo's experience in her 2018 book, *Blue Dreams,* also adds that, to this day, there are almost no studies that examine the long-term effects of any psychoactive drug, or that look carefully over long periods of time at the extent to which those taking them adhere to the drug taking regimens they have been assigned, despite numerous reports by patients and others concerning the tendency of many to "go off their meds" when they tire of the dulling or numbing experiential effects that attend their drug use.

I can attest personally to the dulling effects of psychotropic drugs, having experienced them when, as a student at the University of Alberta, I was misdiagnosed with a mild anxiety disorder when in fact I was suffering from lactose intolerance, something that had plagued me throughout my childhood and adolescence, but about which I and my family knew nothing. Fortunately, one of the physicians treating me at the University of Alberta Hospital suspected the real cause of my stomach and intestinal upsets. After swearing off milk, which ironically was my and my parent's "go to remedy" for stomach problems, my symptoms vanished almost immediately. When I stopped taking the Valium that had been prescribed for my "anxiety," I couldn't believe how wonderfully alive I felt, as if I was returning to a real world of immediate sensation, filled with joys, disappointments and the other highs and lows of being truly alive. All of this, and I had been taking Valium for a little over a month!

• • •

Despite the availability of the new drugs, expanded facilities and staff, and open wards and access to hospital grounds for many patients, daily life on the wards at the Ponoka Hospital continued to present significant difficulties for both patients and ward staff. A few excerpts from Doreen Sturla-Scott's memoir[43] of her time as a psychiatric nurse at Ponoka during the early 1950s give a palpable sense of these conditions, some of which continued well into the mid-1950s and later.

> Each woman had their precious possessions in a cotton bag, made at the hospital in the Linen Room...[from] leftover material...Each patient had one of these bags, so precious, for they would hold...lipstick, a comb, a bar of soap, perhaps some blank paper and a pen, perhaps a favourite pair of earrings, and most importantly, extra food they managed to secure when they went to the Dining Room...Every so often we had to take away these bags...for [they] would be stuffed with stale bread and rotting fruit...Some patients put up a great fuss, others were stoic about it...soon the person would have a new, clean one to begin all over again. ...
>
> The personal hygiene on the ward was accomplished at great effort, but not entirely successfully. No deodorant, or even tooth-paste, the women had to line up in the bathroom in

---

43   Sturla-Scott (2009). *High Hopes – Degrees of Graduation.* Available on Kindle from Amazon.

front of a wooden cupboard, the staff had a key to open it, and inside, their tired and worn-out toothbrushes were each on a nail, with the person's last name on a piece of adhesive... Then the staff would shake out some toothpowder from a tin with holes...All of this had to be done in a bathroom where there were no doors to provide privacy, and was pretty smelly first thing in the morning, and women jostling about to get their brush from the staff before someone else took it away from them...There were no tampons yet, and the Linen Room made makeshift belts for this use, pinning the pads with safety-pins, which were often scarce in number. There were worse trials, I'm sure, but I would have liked to have bet that not one of the staff would ever have had to care for themselves in front of the others. It gave a whole new meaning to a private room, and a door on the toilet. In a year or two, doors were put on but without locks to secure them.

Because the diet of the day was not too nutritionally sound... the patients tended to hoard food, especially fruit, or a piece of cake, in those cheap cotton drawstring bags they carried to, even into the toilet! I dreaded the days that we had to frisk the women...as they tried to hang on to their treasures...But...we had so much trouble with mice, and with a whole new brand of insects crawling everywhere in search of crumbs, it simply had to be done. The mice were the most trouble at night.

Lots of times we would not have enough pillows or blankets, and in the very cold winter nights, the patients would often bring down their coats for extra warmth. Some of the patients had trouble with their bladders and would have accidents during the night. We would try to catch the damp mattresses... but some would inevitably be missed, so the hapless person next night would have a wet and smelly bed to sleep on.

· · ·

In thinking about patient care and treatments available at the Ponoka Hospital during the early to mid 1950s, I can't help but wonder if the somewhat stark co-existence of advances and innovations in drug therapy with a continuance of the general living conditions described by Sturla-Scott reflects the enthusiasm of some psychiatrists and hospital administrators for an easily administered biological approach to the treatment of those suffering mental disorders, over and above a concern for the overall well-being of patients as persons. As I have mentioned earlier, such a privileging of the biological side of psychiatric treatment and patient care is evident throughout much of the history of psychiatry and psychiatric institutions. Perhaps with the excitement of wielding cures such as those sometimes witnessed in response to psychopharmaceutical interventions, the more mundane, tedious and difficult work of ensuring the day-to-day comfort and well-being of all patients received less psychiatric and administrative attention.

Nonetheless, it also is important to emphasize that psychiatric work in large institutions like Ponoka did not afford the luxury of time and individual focus available to psychiatrists and psychotherapists working in private medical practices outside of institutional settings. Even those generally critical of psychiatric diagnoses and treatments, like contemporary psychotherapist Gary Greenberg, acknowledge the compelling differences with respect to treatment options that distinguish institutional psychiatry from the psychiatry and psychology of private practice.[44]

> While institutional psychiatrists are treating the floridly psychotic, the raving manic, the suicidal and the catatonic and the delirious, we [private practitioners], by and large, get to minister to the walking wounded,...talking...with our

---

44   Gary Greenberg (2013). *The Book of Woe: The DSM and the Unmaking of Psychiatry.* New York: Blue Rider Press, pp. 355.

patients about the meaning of life...[while they] are making momentous decisions about whether a man who thinks his bones have been sucked out of him is bipolar or schizophrenic and which drugs to prescribe.

• • •

With the advent of seemingly successful drug therapy by the mid-fifties, Dr. Michie's annual reports began to reflect a significant push by Alberta's and Canada's mental health authorities to escalate the treatment of psychiatric patients in ways that would dramatically reduce the length of time that patients spent in institutions like Ponoka. In the conclusion to his 1956 report, Michie draws a comparison between 1936 and 1956, a period that he notes coincides with the employment at Ponoka of "highly skilled Nursing staff" trained at the School of Nursing located on the Hospital grounds. "It is interesting to note that at the beginning of that twenty-year period the discharge rate was approximately sixty per cent of admissions, and that over the intervening years, this rate has gradually increased to approximately eighty per cent in 1956...furthermore, in 1956, sixty per cent of the patients who were discharged spent less than three months in Hospital." Elsewhere in this report, he makes several remarks that seem to tie such changes not only to better educated nursing staff, but also to "modifications in keeping with current trends in therapy," noting that:

> There was a marked decrease in the use of electroshock therapy. The tranquilizing drugs were utilized to a greater degree. They contributed greatly toward the improvement in the general behaviour and feeling of well-being among the patients on the continued treatment wards. The drugs also greatly alleviated the symptoms of the recently admitted and acutely ill patients. There was a low incidence of undesirable side effects from the use of tranquilizing drugs.

Michie also describes a reduction in the use of hydrotherapy and "an increasing utilization of group psychotherapy with benefit to a larger number of patients," as well as reporting that "Five units of the Hospital were operated as open wards, and approximately one-third of all patients in residence had ground privileges." Occupational and recreational therapy continued to involve a large number of patients on both closed and open wards, with "The main studios...in continual use," as were "a variety of [other] facilities...maintained at other points in the Hospital," including "a small Occupational Therapy shop [that] was established at Farm Dormitory Two." Also of note was an increase in the number of hospital visits made by relatives of the patients, visits that were encouraged for their therapeutic benefit to patients and for the purpose of information gathering by Hospital physicians.

These same trends and themes resound through Dr. Michie's annual reports for 1957, 1958 and 1959, during which time additional new drugs (both tranquilizing and antidepressant) were introduced and widely used. Electroshock therapy continued to be sharply reduced. Seclusion of dangerously violent patients in side wards was also reduced. By the end of the 1950s, over half of the patients were on open wards. More varieties of group psychotherapy and occupational and recreational therapy were introduced to an ever-increasing number of patients. With more patients being admitted and even more discharged than ever before, Michie's 1959 annual report concluded with the following statements emphasizing change and renewal at the Hospital.

For some years, and in the light of new therapeutic agents, a changing pattern in the operation of the hospital has been apparent. This was emphasized in the past year. The number of admissions was the highest on record. This did not necessarily mean an increase in the incidence of mental illness, but more likely greater utilization of the hospital by those in need. There was an increase in the public interest in the treatment facilities. The discharge rate also was higher than ever before, and many of those discharged had spent long periods in the hospital. There was a definite increase in the number admitted who were suffering from the disorders associated with senility, and in this group, only continued care could be anticipated. It seemed fairly apparent that the turnover of patients at this hospital was increasing. There were still those admitted, however, suffering from organic disorders, and profound psychogenic disturbances, who will require long term or permanent hospitalization, unless more effective therapeutic agents are discovered.

Clearly, things were changing at the Provincial Mental Hospital Alberta. Mostly due to the widespread use of psychopharmaceutical drugs, by the end of the 1950s the overall patient population of the Hospital had dropped to just over 1,000 patients, many more of whom were suffering from mental disturbances associated with aging, disease and injuries to the brain. For others remaining at the Hospital, a much wider array of treatment options was now available than ever before. Patient freedom of movement and social interactivity were increased greatly through a combination of group, occupational and recreational therapies, open wards and ground and day passes.

. . .

An interesting account of a seemingly mundane, yet actually quite profound, indication of improved patient life at the Ponoka Hospital comes from a memoir provided by an unknown employee who worked as a recreational therapist at Ponoka during the 1950s:

In 1950 patients came to recreation functions under all sorts of conditions [and in] all sorts of clothing...They arrived in one size 10 boot, no lace and one size 12 with lace, no buttons, torn shirts, etc. Now they arrive in good clothing, well kept and clean, and change into running shoes, and after they return to the ward they have an opportunity to take a shower and change. The ladies, who once arrived in ward dresses, now

in slacks wherever possible, and one enterprising ward purchased material and made their own physical training suits.[45]

Clearly, more than the new drug therapies had changed at the
Ponoka Hospital during the 1950s. There also can be little doubt
that significant improvements to patient treatment and care had been
achieved from the early to the later years of the decade.

• • •

The same could be said about improvements in the physical plant of
the Hospital during the later 1950s, which included the completion of
a new residence for male staff, Jubilee Hall (in January, 1956), the complete re-wiring of the Hospital's electrical grid to alternating current,
the installation of new machinery in a new cannery, the construction of
a new residence for medical staff in 1957, an addition to the main recreation hall in 1958, and an addition to the Male 12 building, as well as
a new Nurses' Residence in 1959. The last was much needed given that
the eight-week course in Psychiatric Nursing for students from General
Hospital Schools of Nursing throughout the Province of Alberta now
had an annual, albeit rotating, enrolment of 131 student nurses.

The staff increases and new and improved residences and recreational facilities for nurses and male psychiatric nurses, as well as other
staff, afforded a much enhanced social and recreational life for many to
enjoy in their non-working hours at the Hospital. Staff morale is always
important in the efficient and humane functioning of any institution,
but perhaps especially in psychiatric contexts in which unpredictable,
uncommon and sometimes upsetting events may occur frequently.
Consequently, Medical Superintendents at Ponoka typically did their
best to ensure that all staff enjoyed whatever social and recreational
facilities and opportunities were and could be made available.

---

45   Document found in the archives of the Fort Ostell Museum, with no indication of au-
      thorship.

Annual bazaars and fetes, such as the staff Christmas party, not only raised funds for hospital causes, but created social opportunities for staff to mix with patients, each other and members of the surrounding community. More frequent parties, dances, sporting events and other entertainments were encouraged and supported by the Hospital's administrators and many staff entered enthusiastically into the preparations and celebrations these activities required and made available. By the mid 1950s, the Hospital grounds included two well-maintained and scenically-placed shale tennis courts, soccer and softball pitches, a skating rink, a curling clubhouse and several sheets of ice, a billiards room and other amenities. The Hospital soccer team during these days was very successful and well-respected throughout the Province of Alberta. All these events and activities allowed administrators, physicians, nursing staff, attendants and an increasingly large cohort of ancillary and support staff (who worked in the laundry, cannery, bake shop, kitchen, gardens, laboratory, business office, farm, physical plant, housekeeping department and hospital stores) to mingle and exchange pleasantries and sometimes perspectives that encouraged greater consideration of each other's roles, obligations and pressures.

Of course, the bi-monthly arrivals of cohorts of student nurses from various parts of the Province were much anticipated by many, especially some unmarried staff and residents of the town of Ponoka. In my youth, it was extremely rare to encounter any Ponokan between the ages of eighteen and thirty, who resided in the town during the time the Nursing School operated at the Hospital, who could not recall graduation parties, hospital dances and other social gatherings where unattached nurses and their admirers enjoyed themselves—liaisons that not infrequently resulted in marriages and long-term friendships. My brother-in-law and several friends can be counted amongst those who are happily married to nurses who completed their psychiatric training at the Ponoka Hospital School of Nursing.

• • •

Despite the dating, partying and socializing that attracted hospital interns and staff, as well as other residents of Ponoka, the Town and Hospital moved in separate orbits. Although it was the largest employer in the community, the Hospital remained a mostly unfamiliar and somewhat mysterious place to most Ponokans. This sense of separation undoubtedly can be attributed to a disinclination on the part of many residents to be too closely associated with an institution that, despite its many attempts at outreach to, and education of, the local and pro-vincial citizenry, never entirely escaped traditional connotations of asylum lore and reputation. However, even as a child, I realized that things ran deeper than this.

Although my mother, as a teacher and school principal, was active in many local groups and had a wide range of friends and acquain-tances, most of my parents' closest friends, especially "couples friends," other than members of their immediate families, were employed at the Hospital. On our street in the Riverside section of Ponoka, which lay between the town centre and the Hospital, many of the houses were owned and occupied by Hospital staff. Since most of the psychiatrists and their families lived on the Hospital grounds, our neighbours tended to be psychiatric nurses, support staff like my father, and the occasional psychologist or mid to lower-level administrator. For many of the kids I played with in Riverside, the Hospital was as familiar as it was to me. Patients on day passes were a common sight in our neighbourhood, often doing yard work, and sometimes being invited home for lunch or supper by our parents. Yet, outside of Riverside, I seldom found occa-sion to talk about or refer to the Hospital at all.

A good example of what I mean is the annual Hospital Staff Christmas Party. In my part of town, the excitement of kids would build for weeks prior to this event, but at school or in the rest of town, few had any knowledge or experience of this annual highlight. As the late afternoon of the great day arrived, my mother, father and I would drive to the Hospital and park near the Admissions Building, which housed the large room where the staff Christmas party would be held.

My father barely got home from a full workday, preparing breads and desserts for the evening festivities, in time to change into a suit and tie or festive sweater. My mother just had time to change and powder after a full day of teaching and administrating. On entering the Admissions Building, we were met with lights and decorations appropriate to the Season. Aromas of roasted turkeys and hams were underlain by hints of the seemingly incorrigible, "hospital smell." While my parents located the table at which we would sit, I searched about for other kids I knew from our neighbourhood and from school, including some I did not know well (mostly Catholic children who attended the "separate school" in town), but had met at previous get-togethers at the Hospital or seen about town. On entering the dining area, we kids were welcomed by a very convincing Santa who sat ready to receive each of us with a large bag full of toys and treats from which we could choose at least one striped candy cane and a small toy, often a tiny toy car or truck for boys and a small doll or stuffed animal for girls.

After the excitement of receiving our treats and finding our friends, we would return to our parents' tables at the clinking of a glass, amplified through a microphone, accompanied by Dr. Michie clearing his throat before welcoming us to this important Hospital Christmas tradition. The meal was then served by patients, supervised by members of the Hospital Kitchen staff who had drawn work duty for the evening.

After the main dinner, with "seconds," had been served and consumed and dessert delivered to all, some staff member or other would MC a program of Christmas skits and carols, punctuated by brief remarks from a few senior administrators lauding the Hospital in general, and the staff in particular. During these interludes, some of the men, including my father, would disappear briefly, returning much energized and ready for the next round of entertainments. Stuffed and happy, I would be shipped off to bed upon returning home, with the party sounds of my parents and their friends echoing from an increasingly distant background.

• • •

When researching this book and reminiscing about the annual Christmas Party at the Hospital, I was struck by Doreen Sturla-Scott's quite different description of how patients at the Hospital experienced the Christmas season.

> Christmas Day was a bittersweet time for the patients. On my unit, out of 150 patients, two had gone home for the occasion. Thus, it was the same routine, off to breakfast after finding a pair of odd or matched shoes, a mandarin orange for each patient, and after the baths were done, and the seclusion rooms cleaned, the patients gathered in the big dayroom for the gift-giving. My head nurse…dispersed the gifts that had come for individuals amongst the gifts she managed to obtain for each person. The hospital gifts were either small boxes of chocolates, a new comb, a toque, a small change purse or a pair of mittens. The noise in the dayroom was something else, all the patients milling around looking at what each other had been given. No shoving, no pushing. Just a bunch of women trying to make the best of a very difficult time in their lives…
>
> It must have looked quite incongruous, the nurses in heavily starched bibs and aprons, all white, the psychiatric aides in blue with white cuffs and collars, and the patients in their faded and torn cotton dresses, lisle hose, and ill-fitting shoes. We had been allowed to put up a tree earlier in the week, and although it shone bravely, getting closer, one saw the broken baubles, and home-made ornaments, and not enough strings of lights to go all the way up the tree.

Sturla-Scott goes on to describe a Hospital tradition in which the Medical Superintendent and other psychiatrists visited each of the patient units in the early afternoon of Christmas Day. They all would arrive "looking slightly merry, for they had met in the Medical Lounge before beginning their tour of twenty-four wards." Sturla-Scott recalls how "Patients cat-called at some of the doctors that they knew, trying to get them to stop and talk, but [most of] the doctors seemed uncomfortable, stayed very close to one another, and their "Merry Christmases" were more forced, and not a heartfelt greeting." Fortunately, she adds that there were some psychiatrists who acted quite differently, and describes one who "would often bring his wife and their dogs" and banter with the patients. Following the exit of the senior medial staff from each ward, "the patients were herded down to Christmas dinner in the dining hall," where they "were all served a dinner of turkey, stuffing, peas and carrots, mashed potatoes and turkey gravy, and mince pie for dessert, with white sheets for tablecloths gracing the table…They needed to fill up, for at supper that night, they had a piece (only one) of bologna, some beans, a piece of bread, and some jello." In the meantime, after all wards had been visited, the psychiatrists would retire to a fancy dinner in the staff dining room, and the day staff on the wards "were allowed to visit other units, and many went home a little happier than when they started, with a bit of 100% instrument alcohol and orange juice in their veins."

• • •

As I think about these very different stories about Christmas celebrations at the Hospital for the psychiatrists, the staff and the patients, I am reminded of the informal but nonetheless strict separation that existed among these various groups of people, especially between the patients and the others. Of all the differences that existed across people in my hometown, the one that trumped them all was the distinction between "sane" and "insane." Despite whatever difficulties and emotional upheavals Hospital employees might be experiencing in their jobs and private lives, they were not "insane." This was a demarcation that could not be broached under any circumstances. On those very few occasions when staff or members of their families sought assistance for some continuing and extreme unhappiness or other problem, they might turn to each other, but only with the strict and shared understanding that whatever difficulties they were experiencing were distinct from those being experienced by their charges. To suggest otherwise was a very dangerous business that typically ended in losses of friendship, ongoing recriminations and feuds—as I know well from various attempts I witnessed in my own home and neighbourhood to encourage staff members and Hospital employees to seek help with respect to their own problems, addictions and emotional outbursts.

Such reactions might puzzle contemporary readers who perhaps think nothing about consulting a counsellor, psychologist, psychotherapist, or psychiatrist for anxiety, depression or difficulty in coping. Many of us now live in a time and places where issues of mental health can be discussed much more openly, where those seeking assistance are likely to be viewed as sensible and their concerns understandable. Not so when I was growing up in Ponoka. Then, there were those who belonged in the Hospital and those who did not, and the stigma attached to the former was to be avoided at all costs. As strange as it now sounds, I recall being completely shocked when my mother once suggested to my father that he talk to one of the Hospital psychiatrists about his drinking and related difficulties. Despite the fact that the psychiatrist in question was an acquaintance and sometimes companion of my father and others on hunting and camping trips, and that my mother was not in any way suggesting my father spend actual time as a patient at the Hospital, I can recall silently applauding my father's dismissive response to my mother's suggestion. Knowing a psychiatrist was an entirely different matter from "seeing a psychiatrist." Paradoxically, such attitudes persisted, seemingly without any sense of dissonance, alongside a widely shared view of the Hospital as a large, family-like community within which both patients and staff were members. In some ways, the more interchangeable the behaviour of patient and staff, the more unbridgeable the status as one or the other. For much of its early and middle history, the Ponoka Hospital was not seen as a destination for locals, either Hospital staff or others, unless things really got out of hand, in which case authorities might act to have individuals admitted to the Hospital for observation, assessment and possible retention, despite the inevitable resistance and shock such actions might provoke.

• • •

One consistently significant statistic that emerges throughout the 1950s from the annual reports of the Ponoka Hospital Medical Superintendent is that by far the largest number of annual patient admissions to the Hospital was "by Warrant." Patients admitted by Warrant under the Provincial Mental Health Act were those who were deemed to present an immediate threat or menace to themselves, others or society as a consequence of mental instability, as testified by at least two physicians. Other admissions to the Ponoka Hospital were voluntary or by Medical Certificate, the latter attesting to patients' inability to function and care for themselves as a consequence of a diagnosed mental illness.

Under the *Insanity Act* of 1907, an individual could be committed to "jail or other safe custody for reasons of insanity alone," if relevant evidence that the individual was "dangerous to be at large" was provided by a "qualified medical practitioner," subject to review by "a judge of the supreme court of Alberta."[46] In 1924, the *Insanity Act* was renamed the *Mental Diseases Act.* Over the following years, relatively minor changes were made to the amount of evidence required and "time limits to the length of detention were specified." In practice, under a judge's warrant, individuals could be ordered apprehended and conveyed to Ponoka for admission for the purposes of examination to determine if they were suffering a mental disorder, were likely to cause harm to self or others, and were suitable for admission to the Hospital. Review panels independent of the Provincial government and judicial systems were added in 1964 to ensure timely and regular reconsiderations of such admissions based on more recent assessments.

• • •

---

46   All quotations in this and the preceding paragraph are from the 2010 *Guide to the Alberta Mental Health Act and Community Treatment Order Legislation,* found in a section entitled *History of mental health legislation in Alberta* (p. 9).

A few of those admitted under warrant inevitably became ensconced in Hospital lore, and sometimes in broader Provincial and Canadian history. One such individual was Robert Raymond Cook. Cook was admitted to the Provincial Mental Hospital at Ponoka for psychiatric assessment following the murder of his parents and five younger half-siblings in their Stettler home. Having been found guilty of numerous thefts as an adolescent and younger man (for which he spent time in prison), and given the brutal nature of the murders, the 23-year-old Cook was admitted to Ponoka for psychiatric assessment, but escaped just after midnight on July 11, 1959. After being apprehended, he subsequently (after two trials) was convicted of murder, and became the last person in the Province of Alberta to be sentenced to death. He maintained his innocence until his death by hanging and many have doubted his guilt.[47]

When I worked at the Ponoka Hospital in the summers of 1968 and 1969, the Forensic Ward was Male 12, a locked ward in which, at any given time, at least two patients were secluded in barred side-rooms or cells because they were considered too dangerous to the staff and their fellow patients. One story that was repeated to me on several occasions was that the most mild-mannered of these secluded individuals had once (at some unspecified date) been docile for so long that he was allowed to leave his cell to be reintegrated into the daily life of the ward. Within minutes of his release, he supposedly snatched a hammer from the work belt of a staff carpenter doing minor repairs on the ward, and hit the carpenter about the head. I have no idea whether or not this story was true, but it certainly served to keep me and other attendants on our toes, fitting as it did within the broader, then popular, narrative of the psychopath—that much talked about individual who many

---

47   Several books have been written about Cook's life and death, including Jack Pecover's 1996 book, *The Work of Justice: The Trials of Robert Raymond Cook* (Wolf Willow Press) and Frank Anderson's 2008 book, *The Robert Cook Murder Cases* (Gopher Books).

historians have linked to now-debunked nineteenth century theories of criminal degeneracy.

In 1876, Cesare Lombroso maintained that one out of three criminal offenders was a "born criminal," which he depicted as:

> an atavistic being who reproduces in his person the ferocious instincts of primitive humanity and the inferior animals...the enormous jaws, high cheek bones...handle-shaped ears found in criminals, savages and apes, insensitivity to pain, extremely acute sight, tattooing, excessive idleness, love of orgies, and the irresponsible craving of evil for its own sake, the desire not only to extinguish life in the victim, but to mutilate the corpse, tear its flesh and drink its blood.[48]

In addition to anticipating Bram Stoker's *Dracula*, published in 1897, some have argued that elements of Lombroso's colorful description of the criminal degenerate persist in contemporary theories and diagnoses of psychopathy. A former student of mine, Jarkko Jalava, has suggested that:

> Since the demise of degeneration theory was on the whole politically motivated (i.e., due to the embarrassment over the use of the theory by the Third Reich to exterminate Jews, Slavs and other unwanted populations), it would be legitimate to at least hypothesize that modern psychopathy theory and research has carried on with the intuitively appealing theory of degeneration, but done so in a morally and politically palatable form.[49]

Whether this is true or not, I certainly remember images of just such an individual flipping through my mind as a frightened nine-year-old

---

48 Cesare Lombroso (1876). *L'Uomo Delinquente* (Republished in English as *The Criminal Man*) by Duke University Press, pp. xxiv-xxv.

49 From Jarkko Jalava (2006). "The modern degenerate: Nineteenth-Century degeneration theory and modern psychopathy research." *Theory & Psychology, 16,* p. 428.

the morning after Robert Raymond Cook escaped from the Ponoka Hospital, with the Hospital sirens sounding regularly to signal and warn of his escape, until he was eventually located attempting to get to Bashaw, just east of Ponoka, where the funerals of his family were being held.

• • •

The 1950s were pivotal for the Provincial Mental Hospital at Ponoka and for mental health care more generally. The first half of the decade, despite some continued overcrowding and underfunding, was a time of renewal. Key staff positions that had been vacated were filled, and additional positions were added. There was a sense of rekindled purpose and optimism that attended life at the Hospital—things seemed bound to improve. And, during the second half of the decade, improve they did. Leading the charge of change were significant advances in patient treatment occasioned by newly discovered and widely used psychopharmaceuticals. Use of these seemingly magical drugs was accompanied by an expansion of more traditional treatments such as occupational therapy, recreational therapy and newer treatments, including a much enhanced and better-staffed variety of group psychotherapies. More patients were actively treated and returned to life outside the Hospital. Many of those who remained enjoyed better quarters, increased ground privileges and day passes that allowed them to get out in the fresh air, and interact with others and members of the surrounding community. As more wards and units were unlocked, patients were able to move more freely from place to place and activity to activity. Overall, patient health was good. Families of patients were invited to participate more actively in patient treatment and rehabilitation, and community support for the Hospital and its various initiatives was generally high.

• • •

Nonetheless, institutional life is institutional life, and as such, an inevitably more dreary and restricted experience than life outside the Hospital. As the 1960s beckoned, the necessity of institutionalization itself was beginning to be reconsidered for many patients—patients who, in years past, would have entered the Hospital and stayed for long periods of time. Such was the promise of the new drugs and treatments, that institutionalization suddenly was not the only option for patients and their families. In Alberta, as elsewhere in Canada, hospital administrators, politicians and interested members of the public began to debate the pros and cons of different kinds of facility for the treatment of mental illness, debates that soon moved to a more intensive consideration of psychiatry itself, all in the context of other social, political and ethical upheavals that would soon descend on the community of Ponoka and its Hospital. The sixties would prove to be a time in which older ways of doing things would be increasingly challenged by a widespread conviction that things could and should be better for all people, regardless of their income, social status, ethnicity, race, or physical and mental health.

· · ·

At the vanguard of many of the concerns and changes to emerge during the decade of the 1960s were those born during the post-war years of the late 1940s and early 1950s—the so-called "baby boomers," to which my friends and I belonged. We "boomers," especially in Canada, the United States and much of Europe, have been able to exert enormous influence on the world at large, due to our sheer numbers and the long period of peace and prosperity we have been fortunate to experience. As the most numerous generation of our times, we have dictated trends in lifestyle, cinema, fashion and in many areas of life. At a recent fiftieth-year reunion of my 1967 high school graduating class in Ponoka, I remarked that those of us in that class could probably be placed at the 99th percentile of all humans ever to have lived on this planet, in terms of quality of life. Early in our lives during the 1950s, what a reception the world we were born into gave us, ushering us into a time of recovery, renewed optimism and seemingly ever-present opportunity. Some sixty years later, with our entry into old age, we have demanded and received new forms of sociopolitical power ("grey power"), new services like "meals on wheels" and new products like Viagra and Botox. Alzheimer's disease and other mental health problems associated with aging are suddenly commanding much greater public concern and government spending than ever before. But perhaps none of this matches the unprecedented influence we wielded in our adolescence and early adulthood during the 1960s, a time during which we experimented with different ways of being and acting, many of which had direct connections to the provision of mental health services, the rights of the mentally ill, and even more fundamentally, what it meant to be mentally healthy.

CHAPTER FIVE:
THE SIXTIES

Perhaps no decade in the twentieth-century witnessed such a profusion and variety of new possibility accompanied by reactionary constraint as the 1960s, especially in Canada, the United States and Western Europe. Early in the decade, John F. Kennedy's new-world Camelot excited millions of Americans. Toward the end of the decade, many Canadians succumbed to the charisma of a middle-aged, but youthful in spirit, Pierre Elliott Trudeau. At these same times, many other Canadians and Americans feared and loathed the political and social policies and practices of these leaders, and their reform-minded compatriots.

Throughout the sixties, change and its opposition seemed to define the lives and experiences of many in North America and elsewhere. In 1963, Kennedy was assassinated, and Americans were increasingly wedded to the internecine conflict in Vietnam. As the sixties progressed, popular music retained many aspects of the "rock and roll" of the fifties, but also transitioned, under the sway of the "British Invasion," to more varied and experimental forms of musical expression. New ways of thinking, dressing, living and working together were advanced by social reformers, civic leaders, hippies and a new cadre of celebrities in film, music, business, and colleges and universities. Women and racial, ethnic, and aboriginal minorities began to find their public and private voices, voices that challenged traditional, white, European and male-dominated ways of relating and living. Political protest became as common as national celebration in some parts of the world. At the same time, international and regional tensions escalated on the killing fields, not only in Vietnam, but in Cambodia and Indonesia as well. National and international conflict was on the cusp of boiling over in many other places, including South America and Africa.

In North America, especially in Canada and the United States, anti-capitalism, pacifism and non-conformist self-expression made strange bedfellows with the commercial commodification of these same move-ments. In 1963, the year in which Martin Luther King's *I Had a Dream* speech and Betty Friedan's book, *The Feminine Mystique,* rallied millions of African-Americans and Feminists to causes of social change and reform, corporate America marketed touch tone telephones (AT&T), the pull tab can (Alcoa) and tape cassettes (Philips). In 1967, as Dan George's *Lament for Confederation* was delivered in Vancouver and aboriginal cultures were celebrated in an "Indian Pavilion" at Montréal's Expo' 67, organizers sold thousands of Inuit-crafted Ookpik mascots. Mass-produced Che Guevara, "social solidarity" and "women's issues" T-shirts were *de rigueur* at protests and rallies. Liberation, reform, and their technological, commercial and political exploitation were to define much of the 1960s. In the words of a friend, psychologist and historian Philip Cushman, these "two trends joined forces to create a new dynamic (a striving for self-liberation through the compulsive purchase and consumption of goods, experiences and celebrities)... known as consumerism."[50] This new consumerism also became per-vasive in an underground economy that made illicit substances,

---

50   Cushman, Philip (1995). *Constructing the Self, Constructing America.* Reading, MA: Addi-son-Wesley, p. 244.

especially marijuana (but also LSD, peyote and psilocybin mush-rooms), and many prescription drugs readily available to those seeking them.

In short, during the 1960s, self-expression, experimentation and social reform became oddly intertwined with new ways of industrial production and marketing, in both mainstream and niche economies, legal or not. It was no accident that many of us 1960s university students morphed into week-end hippies, wearing similarly styled and captioned clothing, while voicing our demands to have our uniquely creative capability and non-conformism respected. From the mid-sixties to the end of the decade, many people would increasingly define themselves as seekers for identity and meaning in their existence, while simultaneously and aggressively pursuing their self-interest in both traditional and progressive ways. In all of this, psychology and psychiatry became paradoxically reviled and revered for their perceived roles and potentials for inhibiting and expanding this mixed, existential quest.

• • •

In the previous chapter, considerable emphasis was placed on the institutional effects of the production and distribution of psycho-pharmaceutical drugs during the 1950s for use in psychiatric facilities like the Ponoka Hospital. The main story-line of this chapter is how the Alberta Hospital Ponoka, its patients and staff experienced the vicissitudes of increasingly rapid change that included further psycho-pharmaceutical and psychotherapeutic transformation in the context of broader social and political debates and disruptions. This is a story that unfolds through a discussion of the annual reports of the Medical Superintendents of the Alberta Hospital Ponoka from 1960-1969, interspersed with several pocket histories, first-person accounts and personal memories. Significant events and changes include the anti-psychiatry movement of the 1960s, the rapid growth and proliferation of group psychotherapy, a dramatic increase in social psychological support services for reintegrating institutional patients into life outside the institution, a new wave of concern for patient rights and grievances, and the arrival of new political and economic strategies for managing government finances and services. By the end of the 1960s, a sea change was unleashed that in the not-too-distant future was to alter the entire course of care for the mentally ill in Alberta and elsewhere—a revolution that would eventually witness the end of large institutional psychiatry, for better and for worse. In the summers of 1968 and 1969, I was a first-person witness to many of the events and occurrences described in this chapter.

Some of the most notable changes that occurred at the Alberta Hospital Ponoka during the 1960s might be described as reflecting sociocultural changes concerning the ways in which governments, societies and communities treated their citizens. Particularly important in this regard were attempts by various branches of government to work more closely with advocacy groups and community-based agencies to coordinate mental health services for the citizens of Alberta, with the aim of achieving better outcomes in more financially efficient ways. Such collaborations also resulted in the implementation of the Alberta Mental Health Act in 1965. Not only did this Act encourage voluntary patient admissions and spell out procedures that were to be followed for admitting patients by medical certificate, it also included the formation of an Appeal Board to hear patients' concerns, and more generally attempted to safeguard patient rights, with the goal of ensuring that no patient should be confined without sufficient evidential justification.

Further efforts to improve mental health services in the Province of Alberta included an inquiry undertaken at the behest of the Provincial Government by psychologist William Robert Nelson Blair in 1967. In his published report in 1969, Blair recommended greater proactive recruitment of mental health professionals, more and better treatment of individuals suffering from addictions, the establishment of psychiatric clinics at the Province's universities, and doing more to combat continuing stigmas surrounding the mentally ill. Blair also outlined and anticipated a shift toward deinstitutionalization, accompanied by improved and coordinated care in regional systems of non-institutional mental health services. Blair's vision proved influential several years later when a newly elected Conservative government led by Peter Lougheed undertook a major revamping of the Province's mental health services. Lougheed had a personal interest in mental health. His mother had been a patient at Ponoka when she suffered a major depression.

• • •

As early as 1963, the Ponoka Hospital had anticipated Blair's concern about treating those suffering from addiction by establishing a formal program for the treatment of alcoholism. This treatment initiative was developed and offered in cooperation with the Alcoholism Foundation of Alberta and members of Alcoholics Anonymous. The results of its first year of operation were summarized by Dr. Michie in his 1963 annual report as "encouraging. The main difficulty encountered was the excessive number who sought admission to the hospital for participation in the program." In subsequent years, many more sufferers from alcohol and substance abuse were admitted to the Hospital, but demand continued to outstrip possible intake. In addition to didactic lectures and general supervision and planning of treatments with patients and their families, a particularly noteworthy method adopted in the treatment of addicted patients was extensive use of group therapy, not only including patients, but also with the families of those undergoing treatment. Selected members of the nursing staff were recruited and trained to work in this program under the general supervision of one of the Hospital staff physicians. Finally, there was a treatment program in place at our hometown Hospital for people like my father. However, he was not one of those queuing for treatment.

• • •

Throughout the 1960s, the Hospital continued to expand and diversify its programs of group psychotherapy. Other than the administration of psychopharmaceuticals, this was by far the most frequently employed active treatment offered to patients at the Hospital. By the end of the 1960s, the AHP had established itself as a leading institution in the offering of group therapy. The first group process workshop in the Province of Alberta was hosted by the Ponoka Hospital, with subsequent meetings held in Banff and Jasper.[51] These "institutes" focused on the theory and practice of group psychotherapy, but also included interpersonal encounters, using methods and practices introduced by psychologists Carl Rogers, Fritz Perls and others associated with the "encounter group movement" at places like La Jolla and Big Sur along the California coast.

So committed were the administration and staff of the Ponoka Hospital to psychotherapy (individual and group) that when I first worked there in the Summer of 1968 as a temporary institutional attendant, part of our job orientation was to watch films of Rogers, Perls and rational-emotive therapist Albert Ellis, each conducting therapeutic interviews with a client whose name was Gloria.[52] I subsequently studied these and other similar films in depth as a graduate student at the University of Alberta and used them in my own courses on psychotherapy and the history of psychology at The University of Western Ontario (UWO) and Simon Fraser University.

• • •

While at UWO, I became more seriously interested in Albert Ellis' rational-emotive therapy. Having published a research article that supported certain aspects of Ellis' approach, I was invited by him to spend a weekend at his New York Rational-Emotive Institute housed

---

51   See Earl Roberts' history of the Alberta Hospital Ponoka (p. 203-204) in *Ponoka Panorama*, 1973.

52   Her full name was Gloria Szymanski. She had agreed to be filmed having a single therapy session conducted with each of these three therapists. The result was a documentary film, *Three Approaches to Psychotherapy*, produced by Psychedfilms in 1965.

on the lower floors of a large Upper Eastside Manhattan townhouse, which also contained his private residence on the top levels. So popular was Ellis' approach to group psychotherapy that on Friday evenings he opened a large ground-level room to anyone who wanted to "drop in" for a group therapy session with him as group leader. In his letter to me dated October 16, 1984, Ellis described his therapeutic approach: "The main theory of RET [Rational-Emotive Therapy] says that when humans rigidly take their preferences and escalate them into absolutistic musts they become emotionally disturbed." In the interactions I witnessed during my visit, Ellis repeatedly zeroed in on participants' comments in which he detected such escalations. For example, when group members became or reported themselves as emotionally upset by what they regarded as hurtful or dismissive comments or behaviors from others, he would ask them if they believed they must never be offended or hurt. Eventually several such instances would accumulate to a point where Ellis would explain that it was irrational to insist that others never behave in hurtful ways and to get worked up unduly by such occurrences. "By insisting that we must never be insulted or upset, we only increase the likelihood that we will feel insulted or upset. Once we put aside this irrational insistence, we can think more clearly about how to respond or if indeed a response is warranted at all."

Although there are aspects of directive therapies like RET that differ dramatically from other, more non-directive therapeutic approaches, the combination of listening to participants concerns and reframing them in ways that offer alternative ways of thinking and acting is common to many forms of group work. Group psychotherapy often is thought to be superior to individual psychotherapy because in addition to learning from one's own exchanges with the therapist, participants also can learn from observing and listening to interactions involving other group members. Oftentimes, as treatment progresses, participants also may gain experience in helping each other. Of course, benefitting from such treatments obviously requires that those participating are able to focus with some degree of clarity on their thoughts and actions, describe them with a certain accuracy, and attend to and comprehend what others are saying to them. When such requirements are impaired in some way, perhaps by illness or effects of pharmaceuticals, possible therapeutic benefits are likely to be diminished.

• • •

Consistent with his interest in innovation in institutional psychiatry, Superintendent Michie was committed to developing group psychotherapy at the AHP, as was his successor, Dr. Byers. Both men ensured that the Hospital remained well-positioned in the latest therapeutic trends. Many members of the psychiatric nursing staff also committed themselves to group psychotherapy, as both practitioners and participants. Several became caught up in the encounter group movement of the 1960s and devoted significant time and energy to their own personal and professional development through group encounters at various locations in Alberta and elsewhere. In my age group, many children of Hospital employees recall witnessing what they regarded as significant changes in the views and activities of one or both of their parents who embraced encounter, and other groups, as ways to a better, more fulfilling life for themselves and others, although not always with the results they might have anticipated.

• • •

Of course, encounter groups were not the only sixties "happening" that interested Hospital staff, several of whom also experimented with marijuana and other drugs associated with the prevailing zeitgeist of self-exploration and discovery. When researching and writing this book, I was often asked by friends and colleagues who lived through or knew something about the 1960s, if at that time the Ponoka Hospital was associated with experimentation with psychedelics like LSD. To the best of my knowledge, although there were a number of research projects conducted at Ponoka by hospital and university-based psychologists and psychiatrists throughout the sixties, none of them involved psychedelic drugs.

There certainly was nothing remotely similar to the LSD experimentation conducted at the Weyburn psychiatric facility in Saskatchewan during this period of time.[53] There, LSD was researched as a potentially promising therapeutic treatment for schizophrenia and alcohol addiction in the 1950s and early 1960s by Abram Hoffer, a Saskatchewan psychiatrist, and Humphry Osmond, an English psychiatrist who arrived at Weyburn in 1951. Osmond believed that LSD enabled patients, their therapists and their caregivers to better understand themselves and others. In his case studies of patients at Weyburn, he found that they frequently reported insights experienced under the influence of LSD that gave them greater perspective on themselves, and made them more understanding of their family, friends and others. After taking LSD themselves, Osmond and Hoffer became convinced of the potential of LSD to increase empathic responding, and encouraged other hospital staff to take the drug to attain such a therapeutic pathway into the experiences of their patients.[54] I recall hearing various versions of this idea articulated by different staff members with whom I worked and socialized during my time as a temporary attendant at Ponoka. But again, I know of no formal institutional effort to import the Osmond and Hoffer initiative to the Ponoka Hospital.

Perhaps paradoxically, given that use of hallucinogenic drugs in Western Canada and many other jurisdictions increased dramatically

---

53   For the full story, see Erika Dyck (2008). *Psychedelic Psychiatry: LSD from Clinic to Campus.* Johns Hopkins University Press and Erika Dyck & Alex Deighton (2017). *Managing Madness: Weyburn Mental Hospital and the Transformation of Psychiatric Care in Canada.* University of Manitoba Press.

54   In her memoir *Inside the Mental,* psychiatric nurse and former patient Kay Parley seems to substantiate Hoffer's and Osmond's belief in the empathy-inducing potential of LSD: "Then psychiatrists began to experiment with LSD, and for the very first time I found I could talk to them about my adventures in inner space without making them panic." [Kindle Version, location 1574].

throughout the 1960s and into the 1970s, this same popularity generated sensationalized publicity that made it almost impossible to secure research funding to study the possible therapeutic effects of psychedelics, and resulted in LSD being declared completely illegal in 1968. The infamous research conducted at the Allen Memorial Institute in Montreal from 1957 to 1964, funded by the U.S. Central Intelligence Agency (which tested the effects of isolation, deprivation, LSD and electroshock) also contributed to a cessation of research on hallucinogens by the late 1960s. Interestingly, there is currently an upswing of speculation and interest in the therapeutic use of psychedelics amongst many in the psychiatric community. Just as contemporary forms of electroconvulsive therapy are said to be much more refined and better understood than mid-twentieth century electroshock treatment, today's experimenters with psychedelics claim to be better-informed and better-intended than those working at places like Allen Memorial in the past.

• • •

By combining more conventional and entirely legal forms of pharmaceutical therapy and group therapy with a much expanded offering of occupational and recreational therapy, as well as adopting a new emphasis on, and commitment to, community involvement and outpatient services, the Ponoka Hospital began to discharge as many patients as it admitted. In the early sixties, annual admission rates dramatically increased until by 1965, a record high of 1,428 individuals were admitted. Given the increasingly complicated and extensive procedures and paperwork that began to accompany admissions in a new age of patient rights and hospital accountability, these numbers placed considerable strain on the Hospital, its personnel and resources. Nonetheless, by 1967 more patients were being discharged than were admitted, and by 1969, patient admissions had dropped to 974. Even more dramatically, by the end of 1969 "there were 905 patients on the books, 576 males and 329 females, [and only] a total of 818 in actual residence."[55] How had these dramatic changes in rates of patient rehabilitation and release been possible?

The answer involves a striking number of sociocultural, bureaucratic, political and economic changes that took place at the Alberta Hospital Ponoka and in the Province of Alberta during the 1960s. First, note that the figures just reviewed for 1969 include eighty-seven patients who were "on the books" but not "in actual residence" at the AHP. These patients were housed elsewhere—some as out-patients being served by the Hospital and its new Out-patient Department, located at the Foothills Hospital in Calgary, and some in foster and group homes located in Ponoka and elsewhere in Central Alberta. As early as 1960, "An increasing number of patients were seen at the hospital as out-patients for diagnosis and treatment purposes." In September of 1961:

> a new service was extended to the City of Calgary, and with the cooperation of the Provincial Guidance Clinic, Calgary, office space was made available for an Out-patient Clinic. The objective at inception was to have recently discharged patients from Calgary and vicinity seen by appointment, and whenever possible, the person in attendance be the Physician directly responsible for the patient's care in the hospital. Eight one-half day Clinics were held in the last three months of 1961. The patient attendance was about 80 per cent of those invited. It is felt this service was of considerable value...The number of out-patients coming directly to the hospital continued to increase.

By 1963, the Out-patient or After Care Clinic in Calgary "appeared likely [to] require extension, probably by...operating one day each

---

55 All quotations not sourced explicitly are taken from the annual reports of the Medical Superintendents for the years indicated.

week," and increases in numbers of patients seen there continued. In August of 1966, the "After-Care Clinic in Calgary was moved to the Foothills Hospital. In November, the full-time services of a Psychiatrist were obtained" and the Clinic was described as a "very busy service," providing "a very useful function in the follow-up care of patients discharged from the hospital." By 1969, the now-named "Out-Patient Department" in Calgary had added "three full time Social Workers, one part time Social Worker and a Secretary" to its staff to meet demand for its services, which by 1968 included "an average of 150 psychiatric appointments per month throughout the year" and "2,899 interviews" conducted by social workers. Also by 1968, out-patient services offered at the Alberta Hospital Ponoka itself treated an estimated 300 patients and made 440 contacts with various social service agencies in the community of Ponoka and throughout Central Alberta.

Directly relevant to the Province of Alberta's strategy of reducing length of patient stays in its mental health institutions was another development in 1968—the establishment of the "Inter-Agency Council on After Care [which] met monthly to acquaint discharge program staff at the Alberta Hospital [Ponoka] with the resource available at Calgary." "Represented on this committee are the Out-Patient Clinic, Department of Provincial Welfare, Rehabilitation Centre, Foothills Hospital Day-Care Program, Canadian Mental Health Association, Department of Immigration and Manpower, Preventive Social Services, Advance Industries and the Vocational Research Institute."

There can be little doubt that enhanced and better coordinated services for out-patients succeeded, by the end of the 1960s, in reducing the numbers of admissions to the Alberta Hospital Ponoka by breaking into the cycle of release followed by readmission of former patients. However, at least two other factors also played important and influential roles: several additional psychiatric wards had now been opened in the Province's general hospitals, finally responding more fully to Clare Hincks' and Charles Arthur Baragar's repeated pleas dating from the 1920s and 1930s. In addition, a strengthening of Alberta Medicare ensured both new and former patients had better access to the greater range of possible facilities and services now available to them.

• • •

Nor should the greater emphasis on social programing, including "Industrial therapy," at the AHP itself be forgotten. This new orientation was assisted by the efforts of individual volunteers, volunteer organizations and businesses in the town and environs of Ponoka and in other parts of the Province of Alberta. In his annual report of 1962, Dr. Michie noted:

> a more comprehensive attitude towards Occupational Therapy. The crafts were felt desirable for short term patients, but for those requiring prolonged care, industrial activities were devised, sometimes with outside assistance. Many patients were placed on a part-time employment basis, and occasionally as full-time workers in the surrounding community.

In his 1963 report, Michie once again made mention of this broadened conception of Occupational Therapy, indicating that "a great many activities were arranged, many of which resulted in small monetary returns to groups or individuals. These projects called for the co-operation and collaboration of many people in the area served by the hospital." In 1965, Michie's successor, Dr. Byers, commented that:

> Industrial therapy was used...to a greater extent, and a variety of articles were manufactured by groups of patients under sub-contracts from businesses in Calgary and Edmonton. The patients involved in these activities were paid a nominal sum for their work.

By 1965, "the industrial therapy program [had] continued to grow, and on four wards a variety of articles was manufactured under contract from businesses in different parts of the province."

Part of the explanation for an increased focus on what was now being called industrial therapy was a displacement of working patients that accompanied the closing of the Hospital Farm in 1962. At that time, Dr. Michie wrote that "The various phases of activity were terminated in stages, the last being dairy production with the sale of the stock in December, [but] it was decided that the production of vegetables is to continue." As recorded by Earl Roberts, "The farm land was sold to local farmers and the cultivated land on the hospital grounds was rented."[56] Finally, in 1969, the vegetable gardens were discontinued, and the cannery was closed after a 1968 growing season during which "the potatoes which were grown appear unpalatable when cooked and hence there was difficulty in selling them to other institutions" and it was therefore "questionable whether or not it is economically sound to continue with the garden operations."

Nonetheless, the loss of the farm was difficult for many staff and patients to absorb. Marilyn Hoffman, a psychiatric and head nurse whose husband also was employed at the Hospital, recalls the closing as "one of the saddest things in our history. My husband was rewiring a building at the Hospital Farm and another group of workers was tearing down the same building at the other end." [57] Apparently, the many changes occurring at the Hospital during the 1960s were not always well coordinated. At any rate, patients who had worked on the Hospital farm now became available for involvement in the Hospital's newly implemented industrial therapy initiative.

The facts that several Alberta businesses were now using patient labour at nominal pay under the industrial therapy arrangements, and that many of the patients thus employed were longer-term residents of the Hospital, indicate that patient rehabilitation and release were not always the primary or only goals of the industrial therapy initiative.

---

56   Earl Roberts (1973). *Ponoka Panorama*, p. 204.

57   From an interview conducted with Marilyn Hoffman and Doug Hart on May 29, 2019 in Ponoka.

However, it is important to note that this was not always the case. For example, several patient vocational placements in the town of Ponoka offered full or part-time employment that aimed to provide patients with skills and experience in the local community in ways specifically targeted at patient rehabilitation and life outside the Hospital. More town and other provincial business operators now were "partnering" with the Hospital in this way. In these arrangements, "patients typically were paid about $30 a month, $25 of which went to pay for room and board in a community half-way house, with the remainder used at the discretion of the patient." [58] Such developments pointed to a new pattern of increasingly coordinated interactivity between the Hospital and its surrounding communities. For example, as early as 1960, "a patients' band was organized, the services [of which] were utilized not only at hospital functions, but also in the Town of Ponoka." As the sixties advanced, residents of Ponoka noticed a steady increase in the presence of patients in their community.

. . .

Another area of increasingly coordinated cooperation with Ponoka citizens was Volunteer Services, a new section added to the Superintendents' annual reports that began to appear in 1963, with the following entry:

> Many organizations made contributions in a variety of ways, to patient welfare. Sometimes these were sustained projects, such as the Apparel Shop operated by the Hospital Women's Auxiliary, with the assistance of others, and the development of a camping area by The Canadian Mental Health Association. On other occasions, the project comprised a specific isolated function.

---

58   From an interview conducted with George Crowhurst on May 31, 2019 in Ponoka.

In 1964, in cooperation with the Provincial Canadian Mental Health Association, the Ponoka Hospital developed and began a foster home program, which, in its first year of operation, placed twenty-four patients in eight private residences. Six of these patients became self-supporting, three were returned to the Hospital, and the rest remained in community living outside the Hospital with the support of welfare assistance. By 1966, the foster care program had placed an additional fifty-seven patients in Calgary, Edmonton and Red Deer, and the CMHA also had helped the Hospital establish another half-way house (The Roberts House) to support patient discharge and integration into community life. In 1966, further support was provided by the Provincial Social Services Department in Ponoka, which began to offer support to patient discharge efforts by assisting patients in foster homes and half-way houses to find employment outside the Hospital.

Volunteers also supported the work of the Hospital's Recreation Department, which continued to involve "practically every patient at the hospital" in some type of recreational activity or another. In 1963 "a camp site in a rural setting, some miles from the hospital, [was made available] for picnic purposes and overnight tenting" with the support of "a voluntary organization," which a year later was taken over and supported by the Canadian Mental Health Association. Eventually, this camp, called Glen Eden, and located at the south end of the first of the Chain Lakes to the east of Ponoka, was opened as a permanent site that was developed for picnics and camping by Hospital groups and wards. Throughout the rest of the 1960s, local organizations like the Ponoka Branch of the Royal Canadian Legion and several businesses in the town contributed funds that allowed busloads of patients to travel throughout the Province to enjoy the scenery of Banff and Jasper, and events such as the Ice Capades and Klondike Days in Edmonton.

As noted by local historian Earl Roberts, the greater involvement of volunteers and voluntary organizations in assisting patients at the Ponoka Hospital undoubtedly reflected a change in the attitudes of the Alberta public toward mental illness: "The treatment of the mentally

137

ill was not so 'Hush! Hush!'"[59] The various hospital-community ties recorded in the Superintendents' reports during the 1960s reflected a much greater government and public concern for patient rehabilitation and return to life outside institutions. Out-patient clinics, foster homes (some of which by the end of the 1960s had evolved to include government run group homes for patients), open wards, access to out-of-hospital venues and events, greater attention to patient rights and concerns, all heralded the sea change referred to earlier. As many patient difficulties yielded to more targeted forms of psycho-pharmaceutical treatment, often in combination with group and individual psychotherapy, and support for current and former patients became more readily available in general hospitals and community services located outside of large institutions like Ponoka, the necessity of these institutions as primary sites for the delivery of mental health services began to be questioned and debated in ways unimaginable a decade earlier.

• • •

Dr. James McGeorge Byers took over as Medical Superintendent of the Alberta Hospital Ponoka in October of 1965 when Dr. Thomas Michie succeeded Dr. Randall MacLean as Director of the Alberta Division of Mental Health. Byers was a quiet person who differed considerably from his predecessor. Committed to supporting both staff and patients, Byers permitted greater freedom to both. The patient population dropped dramatically during his tenure and interconnections between the Hospital and the town of Ponoka, as well as many volunteer and community agencies elsewhere in the Province, multiplied dramatically in ways intended to facilitate patient discharge and subsequent support. A native of Nova Scotia, Byers completed his medical degree at the University of Alberta in 1935, spent four years in general practice and then joined the medical staff at the Ponoka Hospital in 1939. In

---

59   Roberts (1973), *Ponoka Panorama*, p. 203.

1948, he was granted a specialist's certificate in psychiatry from the University of Alberta and was made Assistant Medical Superintendent at the Hospital. Byers subsequently completed a Master's degree in administrative medicine from Columbia University. Dr. and Mrs. Byers were active members of the Ponoka community, belonging to many community organizations. Both my mother and mother-in-law knew Mrs. Byers well through their common memberships in the local chapters of the IODE and Order of the Eastern Star, respectively. Mrs. Byers was an accomplished pianist who often performed at Hospital and town events.

Dr. Byers was strongly committed to granting as much freedom of movement as possible to patients. He found confined side rooms and bars on windows especially offensive and attempted to do away with as many as possible. His daughter Marg Dale told me about a time she accompanied her father to a recently renovated part of the Ponoka Hospital. So delighted was Byers with patient rooms that were now airy, bright and without bars on any windows that he decided to demonstrate to his daughter not only the ethical and aesthetic superiority, but also the greater functionality of the newly installed shatterproof glass windows. To this end, he took from his pocket his ring of Hospital keys and flung it at one of the windows, which immediately disintegrated on impact.

Ms. Dale also recalled living on the Hospital grounds with "plenty of room to explore and play...tennis court and lawn bowling facility in the summer, and skating rink and curling rink in winter for the use of staff and patients," as well as baseball and soccer fields and "a lovely Occupational Therapy Garden, planted and tended by some of the patients."[60] On summer evenings, patients with ground passes often mingled and talked with staff and members of their families in back yards, playing fields and well-manicured grounds.

---

60   From an e-mail exchange with Marg Dale (née Byers) dated January 19, 2018.

• • •

When researching this book, I had little difficulty locating staff and other non-patient recollections and memoirs, but first-person accounts of the experiences of patients at the Hospital were much rarer. One exception consists of two three-page reminiscences by Mrs. Anna Norden,[61] the first written in 1964, the second in 1969. Mrs. Norden was a long-term resident of the Ponoka Hospital. She functioned well within the institution, but despite several attempts to live outside the Hospital, was unable to do so. The following excerpts from her brief memoirs offer a unique glimpse into Hospital life as experienced by a recipient of the treatment and care provided at the Hospital during the 1950s and 1960s.

> In September 1949 I came to Ponoka. I was scared, I did not know what to expect. I arrived at the hospital at 7:00 p.m. At the Admitting Office, the Doctor asked me lots of questions. I would not talk. A Nurse...took me upstairs to Ward 8. All the doors were locked. The first question I asked her was if all the doors were locked all the time.
>
> They took me straight to the bathroom. I was scared and so shaky that one of the patients came and took me in her arms. When I had had my bath, I asked for something to eat. The nurse gave me two slices of bread, a glass of milk and some raspberries—but a patient took them away from me. The Nurse put us all to bed at 8:00 p.m., but I could not sleep. A patient stood out of her bed every minute and got on her knees and prayed all night through. At once a patient started scream-ing—there was a full moon and she could see the moon and she was scared.

---

61   These documents are located in the archives of the Alberta Hospital Ponoka held at the Fort Ostell Museum and Archives in Ponoka, Alberta.

The Nurse took all our clothes in the evening and in the morning gave them all back to us and we got dressed. Then we could go into the Dayroom to wait for breakfast. All the women from the side rooms were very sick…The radio was going but we could seldom hear it: too much noise. The breakfast was good, there was enough to eat, but some ate too much and some would not eat at all. The Nurse forced them to eat. Some of the patients were well enough to work a little; some pushed a heavy polisher, and some washed dishes. We had only one toilet there, and it was occupied all the time. At 9:30 a.m. a Nurse came and took most of the patients to O.T. This was the place I liked the best to go…There we got a cup of cocoa and a cracker.

Three days a week most patients had shock-treatment. Most of the patients were very scared of them. When they came out of the coma they had forgotten everything, but their memory would come slowly back. A friend I talked to one day said to me, "I have had 100 shocks to make me forget, now they're giving 100 shocks to make me remember."

There was so much noise at meal time: the patients crying and swearing and fighting…When we were outside for a walk and we met male patients, we weren't allowed to talk to them. If we even looked at them, the next time we were to go out we couldn't.

When I had been six months in Ponoka, I went home, but I had to come back again. On Ward 7 we had parole, that means we could go without a Nurse outside onto the grounds. I liked to walk in the Greenhouse so much, and the Paint House where there was a monkey—I liked to feed him. In the evening we went to the tennis court and watched the staff playing tennis, but we could not stand it very long because the mosquitoes were so bad.

We had a very nice Christmas concert. We had a good dinner, turkey with all the trimmings, and plum pudding, and fruit and nuts and candy. The patients did not work that day—the nurses served and washed the dishes. The doctors and nurses came around the wards and wished us all a Merry Christmas and looked at the decorations...Christmas and Sports Day are the main events here.

If we had parole life was much better. When we got open wards it was much better also...On an open ward they mean to leave the door open. The patients can even go down town, with permission from the nurses and doctor.

The one good thing they did was to open the apparel shop. The ward dresses had PMH stamped on the back, but the ones from the apparel shop didn't. When you got visitors or went into town you got dressed up. The patients looked so nice when they were dressed up that you wouldn't recognize them.

There is no more shock treatment now (only in special cases); they have pills instead. It is much better in the wards now. The food is much better now. We can't complain about the food. We had a Sports Day in June; now they have a carnival instead. Every ward made a float for the sports day and the best float got a prize.

Everything is better now here. We have picnics and outings at the lake. Every patient enjoys them too.

The changes documented by Mrs. Norden probably reflect improvements made at the Hospital throughout the 1950s and 1960s and perhaps also speak to her gradual acceptance of and greater comfort with her institutional existence.

• • •

The initial hospital experiences of Anna Norden certainly were not unique amongst those of patients entering large psychiatric facilities such as Ponoka during the late 1940s. In her riveting memoir,[62] Kay Parley recalls entering the Weyburn Psychiatric Hospital in Saskatchewan as a patient in 1948:

> At the time, I thought it was the tragedy of my life. Actually, I thought it was the end of my life...My head has been sore for months; so sore it feels as if it has been scoured with sandpaper on the inside. It is very bad today, as I force it to cope with the new setting, the new people, the disillusionment and despair of finding myself in The Big Mental, and with a whole network of shattered dreams. The hopeless weight of the depression is so heavy I can't distinguish the "sensible" voices in my mind from the ones that torment and confuse me.

> Despite confusion, I can read the reality of my situation clearly. Perhaps I should say I can grasp it intuitively but I have difficulty putting it into words. A month of treatment at the psychiatric ward in the general hospital, including some electro-shock, has left me jangled, but I know I have only to lose control of my nerves and I could be the one getting the needle. Displease the wrong nurse at the wrong time and I could find myself blacklisted as "troublesome." I have seen patients dragged off to seclusion or, worse, to the notorious basement. I share the fear and frustration known to all of the world's people who live without freedom.

---

62   Kay Parley (2016). *Inside the Mental: Silence, Stigma, Psychiatry and LSD.* Regina, SK: University of Regina Press [Kindle Version, locations 170-172.]

My clothing has come back from being marked with my name, so, respectably clothed, I am sent to eat breakfast in the dining room. A girl named Lillian has befriended me and there is nothing wrong with her but alcoholism, so I have a well-oriented companion to pilot me through the system. Alone, I think I'd die.

We have no trays and the patients who are serving slop porridge all over the sides of our bowls. A piece of toast and a cut orange are plunked on the top of the porridge and a plastic cup of milky coffee is shoved into my right hand. We sit down at the nearest table across from a row of patients who eat with their hands, mixing orange and toast into the porridge and slurping like dogs. I can't bear the thought of eating. "Cheer up," says Lillian, "The first seven years are the worst."

Despite some similarity in their first impressions of hospital life, Kay Parley, unlike Anna Norden, was hospitalized for only nine months and eventually pursued a highly productive career as a psychiatric nurse, journalist, teacher and writer who has written extensively about mental illness and its treatment. In her memoir, Ms. Parley describes the 1950s and 1960s as "having moved so far from the place I'd known in the winter of 1948-49 as to be almost unrecognizable." "The friendlier, more relaxed atmosphere was tangible…there was a healthier, more hopeful feeling in the air."[63]

• • •

As the 1960s drew to a close at the Ponoka Hospital, it was possible to integrate much greater community involvement and social support into active treatment plans for many patients who responded well to drug and psychological therapies, and to some who received more

---

63   Kay Parley (2016), *Inside the Mental* [Kindle Version, location 131].

refined forms of electroconvulsive therapy. Whereas at the beginning of the 1960s, the AHP employed a single social worker and a single psychologist, by the end of the decade five full-time psychologists and six full-time social workers were employed at the Ponoka Hospital, with an additional four psychologists hired in the summer of 1969 and three full and one part-time social worker employed in the Outpatient Department operating at the Foothills Hospital in Calgary.

The psychologists conducted a full range of psychological assessments, offered individual and group psychotherapy, taught in the School of Nursing, and participated on patients' multi-disciplinary treatment teams. In 1965, they introduced "a therapeutic community approach to patient care within the Hospital that included sensitivity training for staff and patients and emphasized democratization, communalism and permissiveness in staff and patient interactions." The new cadre of social workers was occupied in liaising with numerous provincial and community agencies, enrolling and helping patients in correspondence courses, securing vocational placements for patients, making arrangements for patients to be placed in foster and group homes, interacting with patients and their families, advocating with the Provincial public trustee for humane administration of patients' estates, delivering medications to out-patient clinics and accommodations, helping patients acquire needed glasses and dentures, offering psychotherapy and teaching student nurses. When the many hours Hospital psychiatrists now devoted to working in Provincial Outpatient Clinics were added to this increasingly broad mix of professional activities, it was clear that a major shift was occurring in the delivery of mental health services in the Province of Alberta as the 1960s drew to a close. This was a surprisingly rapid move away from large institutional care of the mentally ill under the supervision of institutional psychiatrists to more community-based care and rehabilitation of the mentally ill that required a much broader spectrum of mental health expertise and professionals. The new forms of treatment and care aimed to provide therapeutic communities supportive of patient recovery and rehabilitation (both inside and outside the Hospital), focused on improving and normalizing the patients' interpersonal and social situations and enhancing their vocational and everyday life-skills. All of this was accompanied by active attempts to reduce the stigma of mental illness, and was undertaken with the explicit goal of reintroducing patients to community life outside the Hospital.

• • •

Several former Hospital staff with whom I spoke while researching this book emphasized the high levels of staff involvement in, and commitment to, many of the changes that occurred in patient treatment and rehabilitation during the 1960s. Adding to the various innovations mentioned here, Doug Hart, a former psychiatric nurse at the Hospital, described the Hospital at this time as

> very progressive...there was re-motivation therapy, psycho-drama, individualized nursing care plans, group therapy, sensory retraining, rehabilitation and life skills programs, and the work we did in organizing conferences and in-service education for staff. We were always pro-education, bringing in speakers and organizing conferences, and never got the credit for being as progressive as we were. When you think of the number of total care patients and the rarity of a bedsore or a skin breakdown it speaks volumes about the quality of care.[64]

Much of the innovation and progressive experimentation that typified patient treatment and rehabilitation during the 1960s can be credited to a loosening and redistribution of administrative and leadership functions across different levels of Hospital staff. In keeping with the general spirit of challenging top-down authority that typified the 1960s, many nurses, social workers, psychologists, occupational and recreational therapists, mid-level administrators, and others initiated

---

64   From an interview with Doug Hart and Marilyn Hoffman on May 29, 2019 in Ponoka.

changes that became integrated within the overall Hospital protocols and philosophy of care. In 1964 on Lawncrest 3, which housed about ninety patients, nursing staff on their own initiative, with the permission of psychologist Dorothy Kraus, began wearing street clothes instead of full white uniforms. As described by then psychiatric nurse Marilyn Hoffman:

> We had no identification on us and our keys were in our pockets. I'd gone up some stairs on my way to L3 and there were three nurses there in full white uniforms. I had taken my keys out of my pocket to unlock a door and one of the patients came over and grabbed my keys saying "You give those to the nurse." I don't think Dr. Michie was very happy about our street clothes. But we did it anyway.[65]

In a similar vein, George Crowhurst, described how (in the mid-1960s) "as a nurse in the social work area I would do things to plant a seed and to get other people involved" and gave the example of how he and a social worker in Calgary

> found a house where we could take in three or four patients. Through a little skullduggery, I was able to get some furniture from the Hospital. We got this detached house in Calgary and got Canadian Mental Health to take it over, and it became Roberts House. Dr. Michie and Dr. Byers wondered about all of this. Dr. Michie talked to my secretary and she said, "Oh, didn't you know about that? That's been going on for some time," and he said "okay."[66]

In his role as director of continuing education and nursing, Bob Reid encouraged staff to take the lead when necessary.

---

65   From the same interview.

66   From an interview with George Crowhurst on May 31, 2019 in Ponoka.

Staff were very open and receptive to experimentation and innovation, whereas, at times, you almost had to convince some senior administrators to try these kinds of things. It always helped to have a least one psychiatrist on board. Staff also resisted some psychiatrists' programs, such as unmodified ECT in which they refused to participate, as they felt it unethical.[67]

Like many others with whom I spoke, Bob described his time at the Hospital as "the best years I had—it was very supportive, very community oriented. You knew everybody. We were friends—the best job I ever had. There were difficult times, but overall it was excellent—the caring atmosphere at all levels of staff—everyone there for the patients."

• • •

Other major happenings at the Alberta Hospital Ponoka during the 1960s included the continued impact on the delivery of mental health in the Province of Alberta made by the Hospital's Nursing School. In 1960, a new residence was built to house the rotating groups of affiliate nurses from throughout the Province who completed their training in psychiatric nursing at Ponoka. New classrooms were constructed in the basement of the new building to accommodate the growing numbers of affiliates. In that same year, the number of affiliate nurses who attended the Hospital's School of Nursing numbered 176, but from 1965 to 1969 this number ranged from 210 to 235 annually. Also during the 1960s, the distinction between female psychiatric nurses and male attendants or orderlies trained at the School of Nursing was gradually eliminated, and the School trained only psychiatric nurses of either sex.

Other than renovations and upgrades to existing buildings (notably the Hospital Kitchen, Laundry and Power House), the only other entirely new construction at the Hospital itself during the

---

67   From an interview with Bob Reid on June 3, 2019 in Edmonton.

1960s—Hopewell—was opened in August of 1964. Hopewell pro-vided new housing for the Hospital's Administration and Admission operations. New residential building permitted on the Hospital grounds during the sixties included two houses and a ten-car garage for the use of medical staff.

In addition to the new programming for those suffering from alcohol abuse, an innovative program for adolescents, The Apollo Program, was established and opened in 1968 to serve the increasing number of younger patients receiving treatment at the Hospital. In yet another example of cooperation with the Town of Ponoka, several of these teenagers attended the local junior and senior high schools.

I recently interviewed one those teenage patients who had been admitted to the Ponoka Hospital during the late 1960s. Now an old man like myself, he described some of his memories of Hospital life at that time:

> Because of my schizophrenia, I thought I'd never be able to think right again. I still feel like that sometimes. I think I was singled out for the bad treatment I was receiving—what they were doing to me was not for me. I was sleepy from the medication and worried about defending myself. Some of them were pretty wild, hitting and choking. Then I got to walk outside and I liked some of the staff. We would talk about stuff. I talked to the doctors about the medicine—it took away my intelligence and made me do strange stuff. Then I lived in a half-way house and was on welfare. Now I live in this place and it's okay. I don't want anyone to get schizophrenia. Tell them that.

• • •

As the 1970s approached, a major problem facing the Ponoka Hospital was a growing difficulty in recruiting and retaining professional staff, especially medical staff. With the opening of psychiatric wards in the

Province's general hospitals, especially those located in larger urban centres, a more isolated professional life near the small community of Ponoka lost its attraction. A likely additional factor was the kind of education and training now being received at Provincial universities and colleges, which were experiencing changes associated with the popular embrace of individual freedom and expression that swept through the sixties. New demands by students and professors called for the relaxation of traditional modes of authoritative education, and more open and relevant curricula that actively involved students in planning and pursuing aspects of their own education, and permitted a critical questioning of existing educational and social policies and practices. In this context, institutions like psychiatric hospitals came to be viewed by many as holdouts of traditional, outdated and repressive practices. A good example of this reaction was the anti-psychiatry movement that centred around Dr. Thomas Szasz, and others in the United States. The initial focus of this movement was on what, by this time, had become a highly contentious issue: the involuntary confinement of psychiatric patients. In this newly critical sociopolitical climate, it is perhaps not surprising that many freshly minted mental health professionals were deciding to turn their backs on employment at institutions like the Ponoka Hospital in favour of vocational options available in psychiatric wings of urban hospitals, an expanding network of community-based services, and what some regarded as the greater professional freedom of private practice. Changes in social, educational and vocational attitudes and preferences further influenced administrators and politicians throughout the Province, creating critical questioning of mental health practices and indecision concerning the future of the delivery of mental health services. Given that change was being demanded by patients and their advocates, by many leading professors and opinion leaders, and by growing numbers of the general public, what exactly should these changes be? No one seemed to know for sure, but many held strong opinions.

...

Early in the 1970s, it would become clear that the new Lougheed Government in the Province of Alberta was moving in the direction of deinstitutionalization, as foreshadowed in the Blair report of 1969. It was not just university and government officials who were now advocating for change in the treatment of the mentally ill. As the sixties progressed, patients and former patients who had become involved in social support groups began to flex significant power as consumers of mental health services, whose recitals of their first-person experiences began to find an increasing audience in Albertans who had begun to shed older views of the mentally ill as unfamiliar aliens incapable of making their own decisions. More and more people in the Province knew something of the experiences, and supported the struggles, of family and friends who had mental health issues. Suddenly, the plights of these individuals were a topic of public interest.

In 1968, journalist Tori Salter[68] wrote about her experiences in the Alberta Hospital Edmonton, where she was admitted, upon feigning schizophrenia. In stark contrast with the various efforts to improve patient care at Ponoka, Salter painted a very different picture of life in the Province's other large mental hospital, in Edmonton:

> Patients not on the work or therapy lists went from their beds to sit in the dayroom. The chairs were placed armrest to armrest, in three long rows and on two walls…Many patients spent their days sitting, chin in hand, uncommunicative, and sunk in deep depression…Some paced the floor, stopping to press their foreheads against the small cool window panes. Others would go lie on their uncomfortable beds after all their ward-cleaning chores were done, pulling their threadbare blankets over them.

---

68   Salter, G. Tori. "Five Days of Degradation," *The Canadian Magazine*, February 1968.

Salter's depiction of life on the wards was one of dehumanization and neglect. But Salter did not stop there. She went on to contrast the "spirit numbing, overcrowded wards where people [were] stripped of both their dignity and identity" with conditions at the new 150-bed Yorkton Psychiatric Centre in Saskatchewan, located on the site of that community's general hospital, where patients were treated in the same kinds of facilities provided to physically ill patients at that hospital. When Salter voiced her concerns with Dr. James L. Patterson, Medical Superintendent at the Alberta Hospital Edmonton, Patterson explained that the Province of Alberta's budget limit of $8.75 a day for each patient at Ponoka and Edmonton made it impossible to provide more optimum care of the sort available in Yorkton.

Suddenly patient treatment, which previously had met mostly with public apathy and governmental disinterest, commanded significant attention and divisive debate in Alberta. Dr. J. Donovan Ross, Alberta's Minister of Health, accused Salter of venting her personal opinions and biases in ways that created a false impression of patients' hospital lives, and said that her reports were replete with numerous falsehoods and errors.[69] Some hospital staff maintained that Salter had unfortunately been placed on an older ward, and had declined to return to the Hospital to tour a new "open ward." They also accused her of exaggeration and bias. In contrast, Glen Brant, President of the Canadian Mental Health Association of Alberta, although worried about the stress and anxiety Salter's report might create amongst current and past patients and their families, expressed concern that Slater's exposé not be swept away by governmental tendencies to preserve the status quo. Brant referred to a 1964 report by the CMHA that recommended that no funds be provided for the construction of mental hospitals with more than 300 beds.

---

69   See Ronald A. LaJeunesse (2002). *Political Asylums,* Edmonton: Muttart Foundation, Chapters 9 and 10.

• • •

Despite sparking much outrage and reaction, Salter's reporting was to prove much less influential with respect to future changes to the delivery of mental health services in Alberta than a series of articles researched and written by Karen Harding, a reporter for the *Edmonton Journal* newspaper. Harding's articles actually had begun to appear a year before Salter's exposé in the *Canadian Magazine*. Having taken several months to research her reports, Harding's first article, "Mental Health: Our Province's Stepchild" appeared in 1967 on the front page of the January 24th edition of the *Edmonton Journal*. Carefully reporting on treatment conditions and the wide-ranging views of patients, their families, mental health professionals and international experts, Harding eventually made sixteen recommendations for reform. These included better funding and training of hospital staff, and more community and general hospital services to assist patients following discharge from active treatment.

Interestingly, in subsequent articles, Harding singled out the Alberta Hospital Ponoka as far more advanced than its Edmonton counterpart, and heaped considerable praise on Dr. David Phillips, Director of Psychiatry at the Ponoka Hospital, for his empathic attitude toward patients, active involvement in introducing new drug and group therapies, and facilitation of ward patient councils. She also praised former Ponoka Medical Superintendent and Provincial Director of the Division of Mental Health, Dr. Randall McLean. The CMHA declared Harding's reports true and accurate, and called for massive public support of her recommendations. In the face of resistance to her reforms by Alberta Premier Ernest Manning and his Health Minister, J. Donovan Ross, who believed the public outcry would soon wane, Harding tenaciously continued her research and reporting. Eventually her reports and the concerned reactions to them expressed by many Albertans, including community members of relevant provincial organizations and agencies, were to meet with a more positive response from the new Conservative government of Alberta in the early 1970s.

• • •

The foregoing events and the shifts in public attitude toward the mentally ill and their treatment in Alberta can be seen as part of an international movement during the 1960s to recognize the rights, and improve the living conditions and lives of those at the margins of mainstream societies. When thinking of the sixties, the struggles of African Americans and women in the United States, and aboriginal Canadians and women in Canada come immediately to mind. These and other social movements during this period of time were part of a broader agenda on the part of activists and social reformers to extend full rights and responsibilities of social membership and citizenship to all persons. In psychology, humanistic, existential and experiential viewpoints gained considerable momentum. These were approaches that championed the uniqueness, potential, rights and freedoms of persons, over and above the sometimes reductive, perhaps even dehumanizing, procedures and theories of behavioural and statistical psychology and institutional psychiatry. In particular, reformers took aim at a number of psychiatric practices in the treatment and confinement of the mentally ill that seemed to violate patients' rights and diminish their personhood.

The anti-psychiatry movement in North America is often said to have been initiated by Thomas Szasz's 1961 book, *The Myth of Mental Illness*.[70] A Hungarian-born psychiatrist who taught at the State University of New York in Syracuse, New York, Szasz argued that mental illnesses are not like well-known physical illnesses such as diabetes and polio. He even went so far as to question the reality of mental disorders, at least as purported causes of the symptoms displayed by

---

70   For an updated version, see Thomas S. Szasz, *The Myth of Mental Illness: Foundations of a Theory of Mental Conduct* (2011). New York: HarperCollins 50th Anniversary Edition.

those having difficulty coping with the demands of their everyday circumstances. Szasz opined that many mental diseases were fictions invented by psychiatrists to justify their professional status and activities. He also claimed that much of psychiatry was a kind of pseudo-scientific cult that had more in common with astrology and alchemy than with established medical sciences such as physiology, anatomy and biochemistry. Szasz's book couldn't have been timelier. It quickly resonated with and reinforced the social challenges to forms of authority that typified many 1960s countercultural orientations and values.

What psychiatrists ought to be performing were not lobotomies, electroshock treatments and drug therapies that robbed people of their life energies and desires (on the assumption that they could not be trusted and allowed to fend for themselves), but new forms of psychotherapy that aimed at understanding patients' difficulties and symptoms as ways of coping with lives that were overwhelming them. Szasz was especially adamant about what he regarded as violations of the rights of psychiatric patients, chief amongst which was their often-involuntary incarceration in large mental institutions, the attempted reform of which he regarded as akin to beautifying slave plantations. Instead of improving conditions at such hospitals, Szasz called for their abolition.

Picking up on Szasz's concerns and proposals, Canadian-born sociologist, Erving Goffman[71] discussed what he regarded as the deplorable conditions that existed in American mental hospitals—overcrowded, oppressive and bleakly soul-destroying. Goffman regarded so-called mental diseases as failures of societies and communities to understand unconventional people and their circumstances. These "diseases"

---

71   Goffman was born in Mannville, Alberta, raised in Manitoba, and educated at the Universities of Toronto and Chicago, before enjoying a distinguished academic career at the University of California and the University of Pennsylvania. The full title of his 1961 book is *Asylums: Essays on the Social Situation of Patients and Other Inmates* (published by Doubleday in New York).

were not medical illnesses, but reflected social circumstances such as poverty, ostracism, stigmatization and rejection. Other international figures in psychiatry, like Ronald D. Laing in the UK and Jacques Lacan in France, joined ranks with Szasz and Goffman.

In Canada, anti-psychiatry flames were fanned further by the arrival of existential humanist Ernest Becker at Simon Fraser University in 1969. Becker had worked with Szasz at the State University of New York in Syracuse. In his 1964 book *Revolution in Psychiatry*,[72] Becker argued that mental illnesses reflect constrictions of personal behaviour in ways that result in a loss of or failure to develop self-esteem adequate to the social and existential demands that confront all people. The inhibition that results is experienced as an inability to love and be loved—in short, an inability to enter into the social world as an active participant, coupled with an inability to be comfortable and confident within one's first-person experience and perspective.

• • •

Throughout the 1960s, calls for depopulation and deinstitutionalization of large mental health facilities such as the Alberta Hospital Ponoka gradually increased. Some advocates for reform claimed that the Province's biggest treatment centres at Ponoka and Edmonton were proving to be cost ineffective due to the need to maintain and add to their many buildings and facilities. They also noted that new psychotropic drugs made long-term institutional care unnecessary for many patients, as was becoming increasingly clear, given the large numbers of patients who now were being discharged from active institutional care within three months, and sometimes much less, of their admission.

---

72   Ernest Becker (1964). *The Revolution in Psychiatry: The New Understanding of Man.* New York: The Free Press. While at Simon Fraser, Becker wrote his Pulitzer Prize winning book, *The Denial of Death*, which appeared shortly before his untimely death at the age of 49 of cancer. See my own *"Ernest Becker at Simon Fraser University (1969-1974)"* published in 2013 in Volume 54 (pp. 66-112) of the *Journal of Humanistic Psychology.*

Opposition parties and organizations like the CMHA were mounting more and more pressure for reform. Newspaper and magazine reporting of individuals like Harding and Salter was firing public opinion, and providing a sense of urgency for change to the delivery of mental health services. Seemingly viable treatment options and alternatives to institutional care were being advanced by many volunteer, community and regional agencies, including foster and group homes, as well as outreach and outpatient clinics. The new psychiatric units in the Province's general hospitals were becoming treatment hubs that provided follow-up services delivered by social workers and others whose work was intended to bridge the gap between hospital and everyday life.

Major 1960s landmarks of change included U.S. President John F. Kennedy's personal interest in mental health reform in the early years of the decade. Having witnessed the consequences of a botched prefrontal lobotomy administered to his sister Rose Marie, Kennedy established a commission that eventually recommended a psychiatric unit of one hundred beds in every community hospital to help ensure access to appropriate and up-to-date mental health treatment for all Americans. Canada followed suit, endorsing Randall Roberts McLean's long-standing plan for such facilities in Alberta general hospitals, and in hospitals throughout the country. Psychiatrists were generally enthusiastic about refocusing mental health treatment to general hospitals, welcoming more modern facilities and support services, but also eying the higher salaries that attended employment in such hospitals in comparison to institutions like the ones in Ponoka and Edmonton. By the end of the 1960s, there were two hundred beds at Calgary and Edmonton general hospitals devoted to caring for those suffering from mental health disorders, and permanent stand-alone mental health clinics existed in almost every city in Alberta.

• • •

However, as more members of the public began to accept mental health difficulties and treatments as ordinary aspects of life, new facilities were quickly filled to overflowing. Costs of patient treatment in mental health units in general hospitals had risen to over $20 a day per patient, and costs associated with aftercare in community clinics and agencies also had begun to mount, far exceeding costs per patient in large institutional care facilities like the Alberta Hospitals at Ponoka and Edmonton. Community nurses and social workers were beginning to experience levels of demand for their services that they could not always meet. For all its promise, the new way of approaching the treatment of those suffering mental health concerns was proving costly in terms of the Province's financial and personnel resources. As a consequence, patients were being discharged quickly, placed on leave on a trial basis, boarded out and referred to non-profit group homes. As these various ways of removing patients from the auspices and finances of the Province's Department of Health materialized and were enacted, it became clear that costs were being transferred to the Provincial Department of Social Development, and often back to patients' families themselves. Under such conditions, many patients began to experience difficulty adhering to their drug schedules, and some began to drift away from families and non-profit facilities, many of which were also operating on very tight budget allocations from government and other sources. The streets of the Province's major cities, especially Edmonton and Calgary, began to fill with many of these "drifters," especially in areas where their idiosyncrasies occasioned little public outcry and could be tolerated by officials.

• • •

In many ways, the years between the ages of ten and twenty are the most formative of a person's life. For me, these ages corresponded closely to the beginning and end of the 1960s, the summers of the last two years of which I worked as an institutional attendant at the Alberta Hospital Ponoka while completing my BA in Psychology at the University of Alberta. Because my father worked at the Hospital as a baker, while growing up in Ponoka I felt free to visit the Hospital grounds on a regular basis to walk on its grounds and occasionally to sneak onto the adjacent Ponoka Golf Club for a few holes of golf. As a young teen, a close friend and I learned to play tennis on the Hospital courts under the occasional tutelage of a young psychiatrist who was doing an internship at the Hospital. On one occasion, I encountered a patient with ground privileges who used an extra racquet I had brought along to exchange a few hits with me, until he was summarily told to get off the court by a member of the recreational staff because his hospital shoes were unsuitable for the shale surface. Frequently, I encountered and talked with patients on day parole or with members of the Hospital staff and their families who lived on site, many of whom I knew through my parents, or had met at school or in town.

I was accustomed to the idiosyncratic behaviour and speech of patients from an early age. My father sometimes brought them home for brief periods of time to work in our garden, join us for dinner or just get a break from the Hospital. I had more or less accepted how they were treated at the Hospital, but often wondered about what might have caused their unusual, sometimes bizarre and often withdrawn forms of behaviour. When I began to study psychology as an undergraduate at the University of Alberta, I thought that working at my hometown Hospital during the summers would be a great way to augment my income and infuse my university studies with some real-life experience.

During the final years of my undergraduate degree, I took classes in abnormal psychology and political science. In both seminars, we discussed the psychology and politics of mental health, following some of the current magazine and newspaper coverage of Alberta's mental health institutions. So, when I worked at the AHP during the summers of 1968 and 1969, I was open to re-examining my own child-hood and early adolescent views of the Hospital, its staff and patients in light of my university discussions and reading. *The Ponoka Herald* published the occasional piece about the local Hospital but for the most part avoided any controversy, sometimes alluding to reports of patient mistreatment in writings like those by Salter and Harding, but being careful to preserve an overall positive view of the Hospital and its employees. As a loyal Ponokan, and son of a father who worked at the Hospital, my initial reactions to the controversies that began to swirl around the Hospital in the late 1960s was to think that the reporters, especially Salter, were exaggerating things a bit. After all, anyone experiencing institutional life first-hand for the first time, in mental hospitals or elsewhere, and comparing it to the life they enjoyed outside such places could not, in my opinion, fail to be struck by the tremendous differences in the freedom, choice and attention one experienced and exercised in ordinary versus institutional life. However, over time, and listening to my professors and other students, I came to believe that it might be possible to achieve less restrictive and more stimulating and progressive forms of mental health treatment and service outside of such places, but only if the public's interest in the possibility of reforming mental health services translated into greater support of government spending for such reforms.

I recall thinking that institutional life was much like institutional food, with which I had become familiar as a freshman in the U of A's Lister Hall student residences—far from satisfactory in comparison to the alternatives of home cooking or decent restaurants, but not bad if such alternatives didn't exist or were out of reach. Despite the various attempts catalogued in this chapter to make patients' institutional lives less institutional, it seemed to me that anyone would prefer an affordable and sustainable, non-institutionalized life. Yet, given the very real difficulties in everyday functioning that continued to characterize many of the patients I interacted with at the Hospital (even when adhering to their drug regimens, continuing their psychotherapies and being assisted to organize their daily routines), I had difficulty imagining how they might function outside of hospitals like the AHP. I recall wondering aloud in my university seminars where all the support services and facilities would come from that would be necessary to reintegrate most patients back into everyday life outside the hospital. I couldn't see how, without a huge increase in numbers of well-staffed half-way houses and group homes, the idea of getting rid of institutions like the Ponoka Hospital was going to work out in practice. Many of us university students and temporary summer attendants were completely on-side with the ideals of the deinstitutionalization movement that was beginning to exert real influence by the end of the 1960s. But the magnitude of the social change and government resources that would be required for deinstitutionalization to work seemed daunting.

Nonetheless, by the end of the 1960s I had decided to become a psychologist. The only question now was what kind of psychologist I would be. Perhaps as my daughter recently suggested to me, it was inevitable that my childhood and adolescent experiences in Ponoka would lead me to a career in psychology, but my direct experiences as a temporary attendant at the Ponoka Hospital in the late sixties also caused me to consider carefully whether or not I ever might want to work in such places.

CHAPTER SIX:
ENDINGS

Within a few years after the 1960s ended, my father retired from his job at the Hospital, I married and left Ponoka, and the Hospital itself began what proved to be a long process of closing its doors as a large psychiatric institution. For health reasons, Dr. Byers retired from his position as Medical Superintendent of the Alberta Hospital Ponoka in 1972. By then, the new Conservative Provincial Government led by Peter Lougheed, which had come to power in 1971, had accelerated plans to deinstitutionalize mental health delivery in Alberta. The government's strategy was signaled by moving annual reporting of Hospitals like Ponoka to the newly minted Department of Health and Social Development, renamed Social Services and Community Health in 1975. Accompanying the change in name was a significant change in the role envisioned for this Department, and for mental health services in the Province of Alberta. Instead of being charged with direct provision of mental health services, the new Department was responsible for the regulation, support and supervision of mental health services "through community-based organizations and board-governed institutions. Direct administration of most programs shifted to...six regional offices."[73]

From 1988 to 1999, the Department of Health was re-established, perhaps signaling a growing ambivalence to the closure of the Province's large mental health facilities by later Conservative Provincial Governments. However, by that time deinstitutionalization had passed the point of no return and, in fact, events after 1988 saw a continuing and even greater eagerness on the part of the Provincial Government to divest itself further of direct responsibility for the delivery of mental health services in the form of large institutional care. In 1992, the Department of Health placed the Rosehaven Care Centre in Camrose "under the *Regional Authorities Act* to provide direct delivery of health-care services." The Department's responsibilities were "limited to overall healthcare policy, providing direction to the healthcare system and regional health authorities, and setting standards for service providers...On March 31, 1995, the regional health authorities officially replaced 148 health facility and health unit boards and assumed full responsibility for the delivery of healthcare programs and services." All the Province's "mental health hospitals, community clinics, and extended-care centres" were placed under the direction of a "new Provincial Mental Health Board." In 1999, this second coming of the Provincial Department of Health, which contrary to its name and earlier instantiations acted essentially to dispose of itself, was replaced by a new Ministry of Health and Wellness. Health and Wellness seemed named to promote a brave new world of health care, and perhaps especially mental health services, in aid of an enhanced quality of everyday community life for all Albertans.

• • •

---

73   Material quoted here is drawn from various reports and papers located in files found in the Department of Health holdings in the Archives of the Province of Alberta for the years 1972 to 1999.

As it came to pass, Byers' annual report of 1970 was the last of the comprehensive reports by a succession of Medical Superintendents—from Drs. Dawson (1911-1916), Cooke (1916-1931), Baragar and Davidson (1931-1936), MacLean (1936-1948), and Michie (1948-1965) to Byers (1965-1972). All of these reports were delivered to the Provincial Government's Department of Health in the rather lengthy and comprehensive manner of reporting that had marked them from the founding of the Ponoka Hospital in 1911. After 1971, annual reports were increasingly brief and focused primarily on operational, mostly financial, statistics. The brevity of such reporting, coupled with the departmental administrative reorganizations and structural changes in lines of responsibility just described, removed the Provincial Government from direct responsibility for mental health services. In effect, intended or not, these changes ensured that as little substantive information as possible would be available to Albertans about what was transpiring in the trenches of the Province's mental health system. When researching this book, I discovered that it was impossible to piece together the kind of information readily available in the extensive reports of Hospital Superintendents prior to 1971 with anything filed in the Archives of the Province of Alberta after that date.

To make matters worse, the ways in which local health care administrators interpreted the Province's newly-articulated mandate that they practice "selective retention" of all records and files also contributed to a general absence of historically important documents and materials after 1971. Many records, reports and files were simply lost or destroyed at the whim, bias and convenience of local officials, all with the permission of the Province.

Fortunately, in the late 1960s at the Ponoka Hospital itself, Recreational Director Bill Savage and Assistant Director Mike Rainone had created a Museum in Room 117 of the old Administration Building. It was crammed with memorabilia, artifacts and papers commemorating the Hospital's history. In 1971, Canadian Governor General Roland Michener was scheduled for a five-minute visit to this Museum, but stayed for two hours, and even then, was reluctant to leave. Michener was not the only one who found the local Alberta Hospital Museum interesting. For many years, it proved a popular destination for Hospital staff, nurses in training and visitors. When the Museum was dismantled, some of its contents were put into storage until partially retrieved by staff and volunteers of the Fort Ostell Museum in Ponoka, several of whom had worked at the Hospital. It is here that most of the remaining items and materials can be viewed today. Without this museum and the efforts of its staff, much of the history of the Ponoka Hospital would have been lost. If ever there was an example of why local historical facilities are important, this is one.

• • •

Byers' 1970 report was a harbinger of things to come. At the beginning of that year, the total patient population at Ponoka was 905, and by the end of the year, had been reduced to 772, with 717 patients admitted (including transfers from other Provincial institutions) and 850 discharged. That Ponoka was the primary initial target of the changes sweeping mental health services in Alberta is evidenced by the facts that the 1970 patient population and admission statistics for the Alberta Hospital Edmonton were much higher, standing at 2,169 and 2,555 respectively. Yet even at the Edmonton Hospital, the changes in patient numbers initiated in the late 1960s were evident, with patient releases exceeding patient admissions, both overall and annually.

Byers' 1970 report notes the continuance of group psychotherapy and psychotropic drugs as the primary vehicles of patient treatment, but also mentions "individual psychotherapy, behavioural therapy and electroconvulsive treatment" as less frequently but effectively employed interventions. Reflecting the continuing normalization and family/community treatment procedures popularized in the late 1960s, Byers also mentions that, "In many instances, members of the patients' families were involved in therapy sessions."[74] Other high-lights included the continuing, although somewhat reduced in patient numbers, popularity of the program for treating alcoholics and the high level of activity in the new Hospital pharmacy, now staffed by a full-time pharmacist who filled 4,021 prescriptions for out-patients and 644 for discharged patients. Many patients located outside the Hospital depended on drug regimens for their extra-Hospital lives. Byers also writes that "all members of the medical staff held out-patient consultations [and] saw 303 patients on an out-patient basis." This figure did not include all those patients seen at the Out-Patient Department at the Foothills Hospital in Calgary.

"A new Rehabilitation Unit opened a workshop in July in a build-ing formerly used as a laundry" and manufactured "paddle boards and unfinished furniture products, mostly kindergarten items." Five psy-chologists and nine social workers (plus three more in Calgary) were kept busy—the psychologists offering "group, individual, family and behavioural therapy, as well as teaching;" the social workers interact-ing with patients' families and community agencies in the planning and delivery of out-patient services. Of particular note was a shift to more behavioural programming by the Department of Psychology. "Behaviour therapy arrived in 1973. The token economy system, relaxation therapy, systematic desensitization, and individual behav-iour modification programs began in 1974." Other new programs that also appeared in the 1970s "included assertiveness training, speech re-training for the brain injured, neuropsychological assessment, and remotivation therapy."[75]

• • •

---

74   Byer's 1970 report is the primary source of material quoted in this section.

75   Information about behavioural therapy and programming quoted in this paragraph is taken from Julius Johnson et al. (1986). *A history of dedication and caring: 75 years serving Alberta 1911-1986*. Ponoka: Alberta Hospital Ponoka.

The various forms of behavioural therapy and programming offered at the Ponoka Hospital during the 1970s reflected the increased status of psychologists as professionals, and of psychology as a science of behaviour. Using methods based primarily on B. F. Skinner's conditioning experiments with rats and pigeons and applying them to human beings, a new breed of applied behaviour therapists had begun to ply their wares in a variety of institutional settings. Behaviour modification programs involved reinforcing improved personal and interpersonal conduct (e.g., appropriate personal grooming and pro-social interactions with others). A variety of rewards were used as reinforcers, ranging from tokens that could be exchanged for purchases at the Hospital Canteen to extended ground privileges and day passes. Unlike psychotherapy, behaviour modification could be used to create entire systems promoting positive involvement and interaction with other patients and members of staff. Theoretically, basic social behaviours of entire wards of patients could be altered, at least to some seemingly positive extent, through the implementation of well-designed and carefully executed token economy systems. I can testify personally to the sense of empowerment and accomplishment many institutional psychologists experienced from having initiated such programs. Charts recording the frequency of targeted behaviours of individuals and groups of patients were meticulously maintained, and served to add an imprimatur of science to our undertakings. Some of us began to view behaviour modification as on par with the psychotropic drugs dispensed by psychiatrists with respect to engendering and sustaining change and improvement in patients' conduct and conditions. It was very satisfying to witness concrete results of one's therapeutic efforts, especially since the methods involved were not physically invasive and seemed more or less benevolent, at least in their intent. Of course, over time it became increasingly obvious that human beings were not rats or pigeons, and that the kinds of behaviour that proved to be most effectively modified seldom extended to the overall behavioural repertoires and experiences of patients on the wards, nor were ward-managed behavioral changes necessarily maintained in the off-ward comportment of patients transferred to half-way houses or released to the community at large. Eventually, behavioural psychologists also became targets of activists concerned that the treatment of patients should be both humane and dignified. It was difficult to convince such critics and their followers that treating people like lesser animals was appropriate preparation for helping them to lead lives as persons capable of exercising their civic freedoms and responsibilities outside of institutional token economies.

. . .

Occupational therapy and recreational programs continued to be important for many patients at the Ponoka Hospital. Picnics and camping trips at nearby lakes, bus trips and special events like the annual Hospital carnival were as popular as ever with those patients who participated. In September of 1970, "an Academic School program, financed by the Provincial Department of Education, was established for younger patients at the hospital, with a full-time teacher being employed." In addition, "Several patients attended the local Composite High School, following initial studies at the hospital school." In concluding his final report, Byers mentioned that:

> The hospital patient population continued to decrease during the year, and with continued efforts being made to place long term patients in Nursing Homes and Foster Homes, it is hoped that the resident patient population may be further decreased. A continuing problem was the recruitment of Medical Staff.

Over the next several years, the patient population at Ponoka continued to drop, as the Lougheed government implemented policies aimed at a "de-emphasis of the major isolation institutions" and "the development of comprehensive community-based mental health services." To facilitate all of this, the Division of Mental Health Services, now within the Department of Health and Social Development, "continued to deploy its staff toward the community." A number of mental health workers, including some of those previously employed at the large institutions in Ponoka and Edmonton, were placed in smaller communities to provide ongoing services "in preference to services provided by an occasional visiting clinic [i.e., the older Provincial Guidance Clinics]."[76] Overall, "the mental hospital population continued to reduce in size, despite a continuing high level of admissions." In 1976:

Community services to Albertans are provided by six regional mental health clinics and their sub-offices. Staffed by psychiatrists, psychologists, nurses and social workers, these clinics offer free assessment, treatment and referral to individuals and families experiencing emotional or mental problems. Staff of the clinics also work with community groups and other agencies in developing mental health resources at the local level... Forensic assessment units were opened in Calgary and Edmonton for people who have come in conflict with the law. Those initially diagnosed as having emotional problems were then remanded to Alberta Hospital Edmonton for further psychiatric evaluation.

By 1977, "at the Alberta Hospital Ponoka, increased emphasis has been placed on a rehabilitative approach with geriatric patients" that included "a new behavioural management program as part of the long-term rehabilitation services available." By the end of the 1970s, there were approximately 450 beds available at the Ponoka Hospital, forty percent of which were devoted to a geriatric program that attempted to increase or maintain levels of patient functioning and "add interest to

---

76   Material quoted in this section is taken from the annual reports of the Alberta Department of Health and Social Development for 1972-1973 to 1979-1980. Compared to previous annual reports filed by the Medical Superintendents of the Ponoka Hospital, information in the reports after 1970 is meager, describing the delivery of mental health services to Alberta residents in general, with very little information that pertains to the operation of particular institutions such as the Alberta Hospital Ponoka.

the remaining years of patients through therapeutic activities." Another forty percent of beds were for patients receiving general rehabilitation that was not related specifically to aging. Remaining beds were available for treatment of those with alcohol and drug problems.

• • •

On October 1, 1982, Alberta Social Services and Community Health transferred the operation of the Alberta Hospital Ponoka to a regional board of trustees from Central and Southern Alberta. The first task of the new board was to develop a blueprint for "a positive future for the facility."[77] The plan that emerged was that "All facilities on-site would be replaced, with the exception of the power plant, laundry and Heritage Buildings...all patient activity and treatment facilities, encompassing all physical, occupational, and recreational therapy services" were to be included. A new 400-bed inpatient facility would then be developed that designated "200 beds for the treatment of the mentally impaired elderly, 120 beds for adult psychiatry rehabilitation and substance abuse, and 80 beds for brain injuries rehabilitation." Construction began in March, 1986. After several years of slow and halting progress, Provincial Health Minister Nancy Betkowski MacBeth used the majority of the Province's mental health care budget for 1992 to speed up facility and programmatic transformations at Ponoka.

When Ponokan Halvar C. Jonson succeeded MacBeth as Health Minister in 1996, he raised and reallocated sufficient funds to finish the job. By 1998, Ponoka had modernized its facilities, staff, treatment and training programs and had introduced new technology, like

---

77   The quotations in this section are taken from *A History of Dedication and Training,* produced in 1986 to celebrate "Alberta Hospital Ponoka's 75 years of dedicated service in the provision of patient care programs, as a treatment facility, and to the positive future we have earned for caring for the needs of Albertans." Those who contributed included retired Hospital staff members Julius Johnson, Norma Kinnear, Ellis Moore, Earl Roberts, and George Watson, as well as then continuing staff members Bill Bissett, George Crowhurst, Shirley Pierre-Robertson, and Doreen Scott.

170

brain imaging. In 2003, the Alberta Hospital Ponoka was renamed the Centennial Centre for Mental Health and Brain Injury. With the commitment of politically powerful individuals like Jonson (who advocated the importance of maintaining Ponoka as a cutting-edge research and acute care facility for geriatric patients and those suffering brain injuries), the drastically down-sized and newly purposed Centennial Centre managed to survive further Provincial cuts, at least for the time being. To this day, the existence of this Centre (as a centralized facility that accepts patients from all over the Province of Alberta) is an anomaly that continues against a tide of advocacy for adequately funded, local community care for the mentally ill throughout the Province.[78] Even so, the Centennial Centre, which now includes The Halvar Jonson Centre for Brain Injury, is a far cry from the large asylum and psychiatric hospital of my youth. It has the look and feel of a smaller university hospital, with many of the bells and whistles associated with a modern, efficient and no-nonsense research and care facility.

• • •

After leaving Ponoka, I returned to the University of Alberta in Edmonton to complete Master's and Doctoral degrees in social psychology, and in 1975, accepted a job as an Assistant Professor at Simon Fraser University in Burnaby, British Columbia. During a non-teaching summer term in 1976, I undertook a post-doctoral internship in clinical psychology at the Cape Breton Hospital in Sydney Rivers, Nova Scotia. This allowed me to qualify as a registered psychologist in British Columbia. Although I did practice part-time as a consulting and counselling psychologist during the early years of my appointment at SFU, the Cape Breton internship and my BC practice were primarily

---

78 See Alexandra Whittick's chapter, "An overview of policy and practice in Alberta's first mental hospital (pp. 185-206)," in A. Loewenau, L. Lucyk, and F. W. Stahnisch (Eds.), *The Proceedings of the 20th Anniversary History of Medicine Days Conference 2011*. Newcastle upon Tyne, UK: Cambridge Scholars Publishing.

intended to ensure I would have a job, given the possibility that I might not be granted tenure and promotion to a permanent professorship at SFU after my initial, probationary appointment of five years. By the time I received tenure, I had decided that working as a practicing mental health professional was not what I wanted to do. With tenure and promotion to Associate Professor at SFU, and promotion to full professor some years later at The University of Western Ontario, I was well-entrenched as a university professor, a profession I continued for many years after returning to Simon Fraser in 1991. I recently retired at the end of 2018 from my position as professor of psychology at SFU.

I decided to research and write this book, my first post-retirement writing project, to fill some newly available leisure hours, and to satisfy a desire to revisit some life experiences and circumstances that had proved pivotal in my decision to pursue an academic rather than a clinical career in psychology. As I said at the beginning of this book, my intention in writing it was to join the history of the Hospital to parts of my personal history. I also said I hoped to inject personal perspectives into my narrative that might resonate with some readers' own life experiences, and help give greater interest to the history I tell. In particular, I hoped that the interaction between Hospital and personal stories would provide a metaphorical site or vantage point from which the reader might think more about mental illness and the treatment of those suffering it. These were my original purposes in undertaking the work that resulted in this volume.

Having competed the book, however, I now realize there is more than a touch of self-exploration in this undertaking. When writing about the various treatments provided at the Ponoka Hospital over the years, I recalled my sometimes stumbling and inadequate attempts to provide psychotherapeutic and counselling assistance to those individuals, couples and families with whom I interacted as a fledgling clinical psychologist. The embarrassment I occasionally experienced at these times was not due to any lack of good intentions. It came from recalling the confidence with which I approached my clinical work at that time—the assurance that I, equipped with my psychological education and training, was well prepared to deal with whatever came my way. For example, I cringe when I remember how, without children or any significant experience in parenting or even babysitting, I had little hesitation in advising new parents who were struggling to provide and care for their children. When I visualize myself directing cognitive-behavioral therapy (CBT) programs for folks with addictions, relationship problems, anxieties and phobias, it all seems pompously arrogant. I know that I cared for and wanted to help these people. What I failed to recognize, possibly due to a combination of immaturity and professional confidence that had been instilled in me by my education and training, was my hubris in thinking little about the enormity of the tasks I was taking on and how ready I was to interfere in the lives of people I hardly knew. How could I have failed to be struck more forcefully by the extreme difficulty of comprehending and capturing the life experiences of others in sufficient depth and detail to qualify to help them?

Of course, I was not entirely oblivious to such difficulties, and my confidence did not run as deeply as my professional demeanor may have conveyed. I can recall having doubts about what I was being prepared to do during my graduate education at the University of Alberta and in my clinical training at the Cape Breton Hospital. The training I received in therapeutic skills and strategies, abnormal psychology and professional ethics often seemed inadequate to navigate the actual clinical cases I took on or was assigned. The ethics courses dealt mostly with how to protect oneself from malpractice. Guarding against professional hubris was not a big part of the curriculum. The courses and workshops concerning therapeutic strategies assumed that forming genuinely supportive and caring relationships with clients was a matter of mastering various listening and case management skills. As useful as these proved to be, I often had a sense that such practices were perceived as helpful mostly because those to whom they were directed had the misfortune to have few or no others who were willing to listen to them and attempt to help them.

When I dig more deeply into my recollections, and the remaining notes and records of my clinical work as a young man, I can find evidence of more second-guessing and discomfort with what I was doing than I initially recalled. With a young family to support, I suppose I wasn't in a position to bite the hand that was feeding me. Nonetheless, I find it noteworthy that I do not experience the same levels of emotional and ethical concern when I think back to my work as a temporary attendant at the Ponoka Hospital in the late 1960s. Yes, I undoubtedly was unprepared for some of the tasks I was carrying out in that capacity as well. However, helping to ensure that people are properly feed, bathed, free from physical discomfort and actively engaged with some or other activity strikes me as an entirely reasonable and necessary part of legitimate care and concern for others. I wish I could feel the same way about my history of attempting to help people as a professional psychologist and psychotherapist. Unfortunately, there still is so much about mental illness we do not understand that I find phrases like applied "scientific psychiatry" and "scientific psychology" exaggerated and misleading.

Within these pages, I hope to have conveyed something of what I regard as the extreme challenge of caring for the mentally ill. I did not pursue a career as a clinical psychologist because I found the work to be too difficult and emotionally draining. Although I sometimes found it deeply satisfying, I also found it extremely frustrating. Consequently, I have nothing but admiration for all who have chosen to make their life work the care and treatment of those of us who struggle with mental disorders. I want to make this clear because in describing the various treatments employed by the psychiatrists, psychologists, nurses, attendants and others at the Ponoka Hospital and elsewhere, I sometimes experienced a strong sense that some of these were highly questionable and unethical, if not worse—especially those physically invasive procedures seemingly directed more at subjugating, even punishing, than treating patients. Undoubtedly, in some cases, such revulsion seems justified.

Given the strains and inevitable upsets that attend working in institutional psychiatric environments, it does not surprise me that even otherwise marvellously empathic and concerned caregivers might infrequently give way to emotions of the moment, and behave in nontherapeutic ways. Nonetheless, in the summers I worked as an attendant at Ponoka and a psychological intern at Cape Breton, I saw only a few instances of highly questionable staff behaviour on the wards. From my own experience, I believe such lapses to be infrequent and to occur mostly under conditions of overcrowding, understaffing, stress and volatility. Having said this, I remain concerned about some of the psychiatric practices of the past, and worry about some of those that continue to this day. I often shook my head in disbelief at the willingness of psychiatrists and others to administer physically invasive treatments like psychosurgeries and shock treatments. I still cannot work out what combination of wanting and trying to help, striving for fame and celebrity, and personality and temperament possibly could have led individuals like Walter Freeman, of ice-pick lobotomy fame, to do what they did. Of course, there probably are as many different answers to such questions as there are people whose actions prompt their asking.

• • •

In an effort to attain and convey a clearer sense of what concerns me, I find it helpful to consider a variety of differing perspectives. In *Shrinks: The Untold Story of Psychiatry,* psychiatrist Jeffrey Lieberman offers a damning chronicle of some physically invasive treatments of the past, including fever cures, coma therapies, lobotomies and the early years of psychopharmaceutical treatment in which the effects of psychotropic drugs were poorly understood. Yet, from Lieberman's perspective, psychiatry has made great strides in the last few decades and he concludes by hailing the therapeutic effectiveness of contemporary drug therapies, non-invasive forms of psychotherapy that seem to be linked to particular neural changes, and brain stimulation therapies, which are derived from electroconvulsive therapy, but use magnetic fields or weak electrical current to stimulate or calm brain activity in specific anatomic areas. Delivered alone or in combination, and supported and verified by modern genetics, neuroscience and brain imaging technologies, Lieberman is bullish about the future of psychiatry.

> Over the past two hundred years, the history of psychiatry has been characterized by long stretches of stagnation punctuated by abrupt and transformative changes—many of which regrettably, were not for the better. But we have entered a period of scientific advances that will produce a stream of innovations more dazzling than any that have come before.[79]

However, others, like psychotherapist Gary Greenberg, are not convinced. They believe Lieberman and his ilk vastly underestimate and simplify the continuing complexities of mental health diagnosis and treatment. In *The Book of Woe: The DSM and the Unmaking of Psychiatry*, Greenberg provides a critical history of various editions of the *Diagnostic and Statistical Manual of Mental Disorders (DSM)* that the American Psychiatric Association produces and stands behind as offering psychiatrists a scientific basis for diagnosing, with a view to treating, mental disorders. His conclusion is that there is "no specific treatment" currently available "for any of the [DSM] disorders" that is predictably effective. According to Greenberg, the "disturbing truth" is that psychiatry "has been struggling to establish its credentials for more than a century…because it cannot make good on its claim to be treating diseases as other doctors do." Unless psychiatry can show that its diagnostic categories map onto readily discernable biophysical conditions, which according to Greenberg, it cannot do, it "will never manage to pour the old wine of human suffering into the new skin of

---

79   Jeffrey A. Lieberman (with Ogi Ogas) (2015). *Shrinks: The Untold Story of Psychiatry.* New York: Back Bay Books, p. 306.

scientific medicine."[80] This general view is echoed by Anne Harrington (2019)[81] in her recent book, *Psychiatry's Troubled Search for the Biology of Mental Illness,* in which she claims that psychiatry's current infatuation with biology has overreached, overpromised and over-diagnosed.

In yet another recent volume, journalist and patient Lauren Slater, who has been taking psychotropic drugs administered by psychiatrists for thirty-five years, offers a history of these drugs, their inventors, some of those who prescribe them, and some like herself, who take them. In Slater's account, the new wonder drugs, which some regard as helping to lead psychiatry into a successful final frontier, are both boon and bane. Basing her conclusion on the history of psychiatry and her own experiences, Slater describes the amazingly positive effects these drugs can have for many patients, enabling them to function and experience some degree of happiness in their everyday lives. However, she also describes in vivid detail the steep price that often is exacted by long-term usage—severe physical side effects, loss of effectiveness over time, and unexpected impairments of social and psychological functioning that seem almost impossible to predict. Sometimes newer, apparently more effective and less harmful, drugs cannot be taken by those whose minds and bodies have become habituated to older, less effective and more harmful drugs. Slater puts it this way:

In one way or another [psychotropic drugs] have helped numerous people to live a life, and that's no small thing. Even if the price has been steep, and the side effects sometimes severe, nevertheless the first golden era gave people back their minds and their days, long hours of light and water, serenity in

---

80   Gary Greenberg (2013). *The Book of Woe: The DSM and the Unmaking of Psychiatry.* New York: Blue Rider Press. All quotes from pages 348 and 351.

81   Anne Harrington (2019). *Psychiatry's Troubled Search for the Biology of Mental Illness.* New York: Norton.

the gaps where there used to be screeches, with the possibilities pure and seemingly endless, at least for a little while.[82]

When I read such differing perspectives and accounts as those of
Lieberman, Greenberg, Slater and others, I have a strong sense that
how one sees psychiatry and the treatment of mental disorders can
vary considerably according to one's circumstances, interests and
where one is situated on such dimensions as "giving or receiving treatment," "controlling or being controlled," "degree of mental stability and
disorder," and any number of other social, situational and personal circumstances. I also can't help but reflect on the effectiveness of systems
of deinstitutionalized treatment and care now available in Alberta and
other jurisdictions for those experiencing mental distress. How likely is
it that the latest generation of carefully and individually tailored treatments described by Lieberman can be made available to all those who
might benefit from them? How likely is it that the unpredictable and
undesirable responses to psychiatric treatment that Greenberg views
as common and inevitable can be monitored and managed? And, what
about the harmful side effects that Slater seems to accept as a necessary
trade-off for what is sometimes only temporary relief?

• • •

Contemplating such questions, I find myself revisiting the story I have
told about the Ponoka Hospital, from its earliest days as an Asylum for
the Insane to the beginning of deinstitutionalization in the early 1970s.
Whenever I drive or walk through urban areas like the downtown east
side of Vancouver (where the ravages of mental illness manifest in
addiction, poverty, social ostracism and suffering), I find myself thinking about my "hometown asylum." Because it is replete with mixed
and complex emotions and memories that often are suspect, nostalgia

---

82   Lauren Slater (2018). *Blue Dreams: The Science and the Story of the Drugs that Changed Our Minds*. New York: Little, Brown and Company, p. 351.

can be dangerously misleading. This is a good reason for attempting to balance one's memories with historical study and research. Having made such an attempt, I find myself asking if many of the mentally ill who now live as best they can on urban streets really are better off than they would be in some kind of institutional environment, especially if funds and resources somehow could be made available to enable a system of smaller regional psychiatric institutions, accompanied by properly planned, staffed and resourced group and transition homes and community clinics. This was the model of mental health delivery envisioned by reformers like Hincks and Baragar, and promised in many mid-twentieth century reports that recommended the closing of large psychiatric hospitals like Ponoka. However, in most cases, such closures were not accompanied by ensuring that the alternative systems of support and service delivery were actually in place. Governments and many taxpayers seemed content to reap the fiscal savings of dein-stitutionalization and tolerate the social costs of underfunding replace-ment services and facilities.

When interviewing several ex-staff who had worked for many years at the Ponoka Hospital, I was repeatedly struck by the extent to which they had become personally invested in their work at the AHP. They often spoke of their interactions with patients and other staff in familial terms, as if they all belonged to an extended family whose members looked out for and cared about each other. With deinstitutionalization, that extended family disintegrated. As mid-level administrator Bob Reid put it:

Staff were very concerned about the patients during this time. We were a family, self-contained, and the patients were part of that. To see them go where they didn't want to go, and losing all social contact they had become accustomed to, was very upsetting to many. The long-term patients who had been there for thirty or forty years had a terrible time adjusting outside the Hospital. Some of the new community facilities were

JACK MARTIN

for-profit and the Hospital was not. As a result, they wanted patients who did not require a lot of assistance and intervention. So some patients were wanted and others were not.[83]

George Crowhurst, often described as the Hospital's first social worker, provided a touching example of the kinds of relationship that developed between staff and patients over many years of contact:

I first met her in a corridor as I was coming into my room, located just off Male 10. Patients were coming and going, when a burly, brush-cut lady patient gave me a big slap on the back of my head and yelled at me, "Hello, you little prick." We later became good friends. Many years later in life, Dr. Philips' wife died after they had retired to Edmonton, and a group of us went up. At the funeral, an old lady with two canes came up to Dr. Philips and gave him a huge embrace. She said "You people are from Ponoka and I was at Ponoka, too." It was that same lady, many years older and without the brush-cut. She had been transferred to Oliver [Provincial Mental Hospital, Edmonton], and over the years had been discharged and [was] living in the community. And now here was this once rebellious young lady who had made her way back into society and still remembered us.[84]

I think it deeply unfortunate that the community-oriented impulses that gave birth to progressive proposals for deinstitutionalization seem not to have resulted in a well-organized and integrated system of inter-related smaller care facilities. Instead:

Since the 1970s, the mental health system has included a bewildering variety of institutions: short-term mental hospitals,...private psychiatric hospitals, nursing homes, residential

---

83   From an interview conducted in Edmonton on June 3, 2019.

84   From an interview conducted in Ponoka on May 30, 2019.

care facilities, community mental health centers, outpatient departments of hospitals, community care programs, community residential institutions,…and client-run, and self-help services. This disarray and absence of service integration has led to a situation where many patients with serious mental illnesses are forced to live in homeless shelters, on the streets, and even in prisons…The ideology of community mental health and the facile assumption that residence in the community would promote adjustment and integration did not take into account the extent of social isolation, exposure to victimization, inducement to abuse substances, homelessness, and criminalization of persons with mental illnesses. The assumption that community mental health centers would assume responsibility for aftercare and rehabilitation of persons discharged from mental hospitals proved erroneous. The absence of mechanisms of control and accountability permitted community mental health centers to focus on new populations of more amenable and attractive clients with less severe problems.[85]

During the time of large institutional care, there seemed to be a clear distinction between mental illness and the problems of daily living. In its original 1952 edition, the Diagnostic and Statistical Manual (DSM) of the American Psychiatric Association consisted of 132 pages, and listed 128 types of psychiatric diagnoses or disorders. In 2013, DSM-5 took 947 pages to describe 541 diagnoses. Most of the more recently added categories of mental illness cover disturbances and problems in daily living. In the opinion of historian of psychiatry Gerald Grob:

---

85   From Gerald N. Grob (2008). "The transformation of American psychiatry: From institution to community, 1800-2000." In E. R. W. Wallace IV & J. Gach (Eds.), *History of Psychiatry and Medical Psychology* (pp. 533-554). New York: Springer, p. 549.

The medicalization of problems of living and the creation of psychiatric diagnostic categories far removed from persistent and serious mental illnesses...blurred the distinction between the needs of persons with serious disabilities and the population at large with mild disorders, and the former have suffered the consequences of a system that overlooked their needs.[86]

As the deinstitutionalization movement transformed the psychiatric facility at Ponoka, several of its psychiatrists moved to new jobs as government consultants and psychiatrists in private practice. Later and currently, the new and cutting-edge equipment and facilities of the Centennial Centre for Mental Health and Brain Imagery attracted, and continues to house, a new breed of technologically savvy psychiatrists and other researchers and clinicians.

Accompanying the closures of large psychiatric institutions was a biological revolution in psychiatry that is still going on. As proponents of such a psychiatry (like Jeffrey Lieberman) maintain, a new generation of psychopharmaceuticals and neuroscientific interventions has helped some of those who suffer from mental illness. However, there are many others who seem resistant to these possible cures, and for whom such measures are out of reach, financially and psychologically. Even with its history of problems of underfunding, overcrowding and swings in treatment philosophies and practices, the Ponoka Hospital of my youth offered food, shelter, protection and, for the most part, concern and care for the vast majority of those it housed.

We now live at a time when there is more awareness of mental health issues than ever before. Many who have access to, can afford and benefit from the kinds of personally tailored treatment lauded by psychiatrists like Jeffrey Lieberman, are fortunate indeed. Yet among those for whom such treatments are out of reach or ineffective, are increasing numbers of the severely mentally ill. These people are left to

---

86   Grob (2008), p. 550.

fend more or less for themselves in circumstances that make it difficult to access and adhere to appropriate treatment. In the words of George Crowhurst:[87] "There are those, the unloved and unlovable, who just can't fit into society. They, too, are human beings and we need a place where they can live with dignity."

To give asylum is to provide shelter and support to people who need refuge. A hometown is for many of us a kind of asylum. Asylums need not be built of brick and mortar. We secure asylum when we reside in a community that offers genuine care and concern for all its members.

Cradle to grave,
it's care we crave
to help us carry on;
its wings unfurled
it makes the world
a place where we belong.[88]

---

87   From an interview conducted on May 30, 2019 in Ponoka.

88   Another post-retirement project, for better or worse, is to try a bit of versing. This one is titled "Asylum."

INDEX

Please note that the italicized "*n*"s following the relevant page numbers relate to the footnotes and their numbers.

MacLean's progressive reforms, 46–47

metrazol shock treatment at, 51–52

morale during World War II, 71

museum from late 1960s in, 164–165

name changes,5, 5n1

need for mortuary, 11–12

occupational therapy (OT) formalized at, 20, 40

opened in 1911, 5

outpatients in 1960s, 132–133, 138

overcrowded and underfunded at end of 1930s, 62

overcrowding 1950–1955, 91–92, 119

overcrowding challenges in 1930s in, 37, 45–46

patient admissions by warrant, 116–117

patient growth and diversification in 1920s, 21

patient population peaked in 1937, 45

patient reintroduction into society in 1960s, 145–147

patients' lives during first decades of 20th century, 27–28

personal memoir during 1950s and 1960s, 140–142, 140n61

pharmaceutical therapy in 1960s, 131–132

physical improvements during later 1950s, 109

pioneering years (1912–1919), 13–15

psychiatric nurses' and attendants' training in 1930s at, 27, 35–36, 47

psychologists at, 54

psychopharmaceuticals used at, 97–98

psychotherapeutic transformation in sixties, 124

psychotherapy during 1950s, 1960s into 1970s at, 56

rapid changes in sixties in, 124–125

recreational therapist at, 108–109

rehabilitation and cooperation with townspeople, 135–136

renamed Alberta Hospital Ponoka in 1964, 5

renamed Centennial Centre for Mental Health and Brain Injury in 2003, 171

renamed Provincial Mental Hospital in 1923, 5

renewed optimism in post-war years, 84–85, 119

separation from town, 111–115

site of, 1–2

social workers at, 54

special treatments at, 84–85

H

half-way houses, 136, 137

hallucinations, 99

hallucinogens, 130–131

Halvar Jonson Centre for Brain Injury, 171

Harding, Karen, 153, 157, 159

Harrington, Anne, 177, 177n81

Hart, Doug, 135n57, 146, 146n64, 147n65

High Hopes – Degrees of Graduation (Sturla-Scott), 23n7, 32n11, 50–51, 50n17, 80–81, 80n32, 103–104, 103n43

Hill, Robert Gardiner, 6

Hincks, Clarence (Clare), 16, 17, 24, 28, 54, 85, 133, 179

Hincks-Farrar report (into Hobbs-Lord-Scott incident), 24, 25, 33

    acceptance of by Alberta Government, 26

    historical and humanitarian context, 24–25

    recommendations, 24

A history of dedication and caring: 75 years serving Alberta 1911–1986 (Johnson), 5n2, 10n4, 166n75

A History of Dedication and Training (Alberta Hospital Ponoka's 75 year dedication, 1986), 170n77

History of Psychiatry and Medical Psychology (Wallace & Gach (Eds.)), 100n40, 181n85

History of Psychotherapy: A Century of Change (Freedheim), 95n36

Hitler, Adolf, 64

Hoadley, George, 23

Hobbs, Arthur, 23, 24, 25

Hobbs-Lord-Scott incident, 23–24, 23n6

Hoffer, Abram, 130, 130n54

Hoffman, Marilyn, 135, 135n57, 146n64, 147, 147n65

Holiday of Darkness: A Psychologist's Personal Journey Out of His Depression (Endler), 76n27

hospital administrators, 36–37

hospital attendants' training, 26–27

Hospital for Returned Soldiers, Red Deer, 21

humanistic perspective toward patients, 15, 55–56, 96, 154

hydrotherapeutic treatments, 18–19, 24, 26, 47, 48, 84, 107

hypnotism, 49, 94

hysteria, 56, 94
hysterics, 49

I
"I Had a Dream" speech (King), 123
imipramine, 99, 100
immigration, 13
Indonesian wars, 123
industrial therapy, 134–136
influenza outbreaks (1936 & 1937), 45
Insane Asylum at Ponoka. *See* Ponoka Hospital for the Insane (Insane Asylum at Ponoka)
Inside the Mental: Silence, Stigma, Psychiatry and LSD (Parley), 130n54, 143n62, 144n63
institutionalization, 120
insulin shock therapy, 47–48, 49–51, 52, 75n24, 92, 94
    combined with electroshock treatment, 84
    replaced by electroshock therapy, 74
    replaced by psychopharmaceuticals, 97
intelligence quotient (IQ), 41, 42
Inter-Agency Council on After Care, 133
Inuit peoples, 123

J
Jaffray, Stuart K., 54
Jalava, Jarkko, 118, 118n49
James, William, 53
Johnson, Julius, 5n2, 10n4, 166n75, 170n77
Jonson, Halvar C., 170, 171
Journal of Humanistic Psychology, 156n72
Juvenile Delinquency Act, 21

K
Kennedy, John F., 122, 157
Kennedy, Rose Marie, 157
Kibblewhite, E.J. (Ted), 54
Kierkegaard, Søren, 12
King, Martin Luther, Jr., 123

Trudeau, Pierre Elliott, 122
tuberculosis, 91
Tuke, William, 49

U
University of Alberta, 4, 12, 14, 44, 57, 69, 79, 86, 102, 127, 138, 139,
    171, 173
University of Alberta Hospital, Edmonton, 30, 85
University of Manitoba, 33
University of Rome, 75
University of Toronto, 17
L'Uomo Delinquente (Lombroso), 118n48
U.S. Central Intelligence Agency, 131
Utica, New York, 8

V
Valium, 99, 103
Vange, H.S., 26
Veit, Joanne B., 42
Viagra, 121
Vietnam Wars, 122, 123

W
Wagner-Jauregg, Julius, 31
Wallace, Edwin R. W. IV, 100n40, 181n85
Walsh, James, 26, 26n9
Wartime Prices and Trade Board, 67
Watson, John B., 96
Western University (*prev.* The University of Western Ontario (UWO)), 7n3,
    127, 172
Weyburn psychiatric facility, Saskatchewan, 130, 143
Whittick, Alexandra, 5n2, 171n78
Wilde, Oscar, 37, 44
Winnicott, D.W., 96
Woolf, Virginia, 98
The Work of Justice: The Trials of Raymond Cook (Pecover), 117n47
World War I (1914–1918),
    savings bonds, 15

ABOUT

THE AUTHOR

The Alberta Hospital Ponoka is the backdrop of the author's formative years, and a catalyst for a forty-seven-year career as a professional and academic psychologist.

Jack Martin began as an educational and counselling psychologist, and he spent many years as a researcher of counselling and psychotherapy. By mid-career, he became devoted to the history and theory of psychology. At the end of 2018, he retired from his position as Burnaby Mountain Chair of Psychology at Simon Fraser University. He is a Fellow of the Canadian and American Psychological Associations, former President of the Society for Theoretical and Philosophical Psychology (STPP), lead editor of the Wiley Handbook of Theoretical and Philosophical Psychology, and recipient of the STPP's Award for Distinguished Lifetime Contributions to Theoretical and Philosophical Psychology. Much of his later career work focused on the psychology of personhood and the psycho-biographical study of individual lives. Martin is also the award-winning author, co-author, or co-editor of seventeen books about applied psychology, and the theory and history of psychology.

Martin and his wife, Wyn, live in Tsawwassen, British Columbia.